ASK PHYSICS-3

EXPLORING THE CONCEPTS

KUNAL CHOUDHURY

Copyright © Kunal Choudhury
All Rights Reserved.

ISBN 979-888629082-0

This book has been published with all efforts taken to make the material error-free after the consent of the author. However, the author and the publisher do not assume and hereby disclaim any liability to any party for any loss, damage, or disruption caused by errors or omissions, whether such errors or omissions result from negligence, accident, or any other cause.

While every effort has been made to avoid any mistake or omission, this publication is being sold on the condition and understanding that neither the author nor the publishers or printers would be liable in any manner to any person by reason of any mistake or omission in this publication or for any action taken or omitted to be taken or advice rendered or accepted on the basis of this work. For any defect in printing or binding the publishers will be liable only to replace the defective copy by another copy of this work then available.

Contents

Acknowledgements   *v*

Preface   *vii*

Part-1 Newtonian Mechanics-1

   1. Basic Terms   3

   2. Motion And The Laws Of Motion   5

   3. Types Of Motion   13

   4. The Types Of Forces   19

   5. Pseudo Forces   24

Part-2 Heat And Temperature

   6. Heat And Temperature   29

   7. Thermal Expansion   33

   8. Calorimetry   43

   9. Heat Transfer   46

Part-3 The Waves

   10. Basics Of Oscillations   69

   11. Mechanical Waves-1   97

   12. Some Wave Phenomena-1   109

Some Concepts You Will Get Interested In   123

Articles   131

References   145

Acknowledgements

This book is the result of the support given to me by my parent, teachers and my elders. I have tried my best to make this book resourceful to every " Science and Physics Lover". I couldn't have written books without a source of education which I get from my teachers, and by teachers ,I don't only mean my school teachers but also some of my friends, elders and my mother who also keep on teaching something or the other at every instant of my life, and so I do to you by writing my books . And, because of this I shall always remain thankful to them.

I shall also remain thankful to the publishing committee of the Notionpress book store , where you can write and share your knowledge with others easily and freely without any glitches.

~AUTHOR

Preface

Nature's bounty is full of resources and we humans use it in one or the way every-day in our life but besides this we have discovered some mysteries of nature too but still these all description are only for a small sector for what actually is in nature. That's why here I present infront of you, some of those mysterious topics which may amaze you and even crack your nuts too. All of the information in this book are at very primary levels of these topics. This book could cover only some parts of Newtonian Mechanics, Heat and temperature and The Waves. More topics of these parts and other different topics would be covered in the upcoming books. I have also taken reference from some reputed book like concepts of Physics, NCERT Fingertips, in order to give you a better experience. Moreover, the book is also filled with some more informative stuff like articles and some intersting concepts. which may fascinate you and enhance your scientific knowledge and skills. And, if I have mistaken anywhere in the book, kindly pardon me.

HAPPY READING!!!

~AUTHOR

Part-1 Newtonian Mechanics-1

Chapters:-

1. Basic Terms

2. Motion and the laws of Motion

3. Types of motion:

- Linear motion
- Circular Motion
- Projectile Motion

4.The Types of Forces:

- Action forces
- Reaction Forces

5.Pseudo Forces

CHAPTER ONE

Basic Terms

a) **Rest**: An object is said to be at rest, if it does not change its position with respect to time and a particular Reference Frame.

b) **Motion**: An object is said to be in motion, if it changes its position with respect to time and a particular Reference Frame.

c) **Scalar quantity**: The physical quantity, which is expressed only by its magnitude, is called scalar quantity. Example– distance, speed etc.

d) **Vector quantity**: The physical quantity, which is expressed completely by both magnitude and direction, is called vector quantity. Example– displacement, velocity etc.

e) **Distance**: Irrespective of the direction in which the body moves, the actual length of the path travelled by a moving body is known as the distance travelled by a body. It is a scalar quantity.

f) **Displacement**: The shortest distance of a moving body from the point of origin (initial position of the body) to the destination point (final position of the body) is called displacement. It is vector quantity.

g)**Speed**: The Rate of distance covered by a body per unit time is called the Speed of the body. It is a Scalar Quantity. Formula:- **Distance(S)/Time(t)=S/t**

h) **AverageSpeed**: The rate of the total distance travelled by total time needed by a body is called Average Speed. Formula:- **average speed = $\Sigma(S)/\Sigma(t)$.**

i)**Velocity**: The Rate of displacement of a body per unit time is called as Velocity of the body. It's Vector Quantity. Formula:- **Displacement(x)/Time(t).**

j) **AverageVelocity**: The Rate of the net displacement of the body by the time taken is called the average velocity of the body. Formula:- **average velocity=$\Delta x/\Delta t$.**

k) **Acceleration**: The rate of change of velocity per unit time is known as acceleration. The acceleration is vector quantity. It has three types :

i) **Positive acceleration**; where the acceleration increases,

ii) **Retardation**; where the acceleration is negative,

iii) **Variable acceleration**; where the acceleration changes in each instant.

The equations of motion

i) $v = u + at$

ii) $S = ut + (at^2)/2$

iii) $v^2 = u^2 + 2aS$

CHAPTER TWO

Motion and the laws of Motion

Motion is the movement body with respect to time and a reference point or **'Frame of Reference'**. The Frame of Reference is nothing but the 4-dimensional system where we consider the position of the object by defining the components of the 'x axis' , the 'y axis' and the 'z axis' and the time . We represent it in the form of (x,y,z)t where the ' (x,y,z) ' is the position and the 't' is the time of the object or body. These frames of reference, based on the holding or not holding true of Newton's laws (1st and 2nd) can be divided into two types the inertial frames and the non-inertial frames. The inertial frames are those frames where the first law of motion or the first and second law of Newton is applicable or holds true and the second type of frame is non- inertial frames where the first and second law of Newton is not applicable or it does not hold true. Now certainly you would start thinking , how does the 1st and 2nd law of Newton not hold true in non-inertial frames? Why? To know that , lets go further with this..........

1st LAW OF MOTION

The **first law of motion** says, that when the acceleration acting on a body is zero the force acting on the body is zero, and vice versa. So it also staes that they are interdependent so , from this we can state that **Force(F) $\propto$ acceleration(a)**. But as we stated earlier that in the non inertial frames , the first law of newton does not remain valid, so let us understand it. Consider a case where , you are travelling through a rickshaw and the rickshaw pilot suddenly applied brakes, but why do then we move forwards? the rickshaw pilot applied brakes (retardation) on the rickshaw but not on you, but then too, you move forwards!!! here the you were at rest means that your acceleration was zero but when the rickshaw pilot applied the brakes a **'Pseudo Force'** was applied to you. Pseudo Forces are the imaginary forces

, which are used to make the first law of Newton valid in the non-inertial frame , just like that of the Rickshaw you were sitting in. Fig.1 shows you the whole event, where the pseudo force is 'F' and the force of the brakes is 'S' .

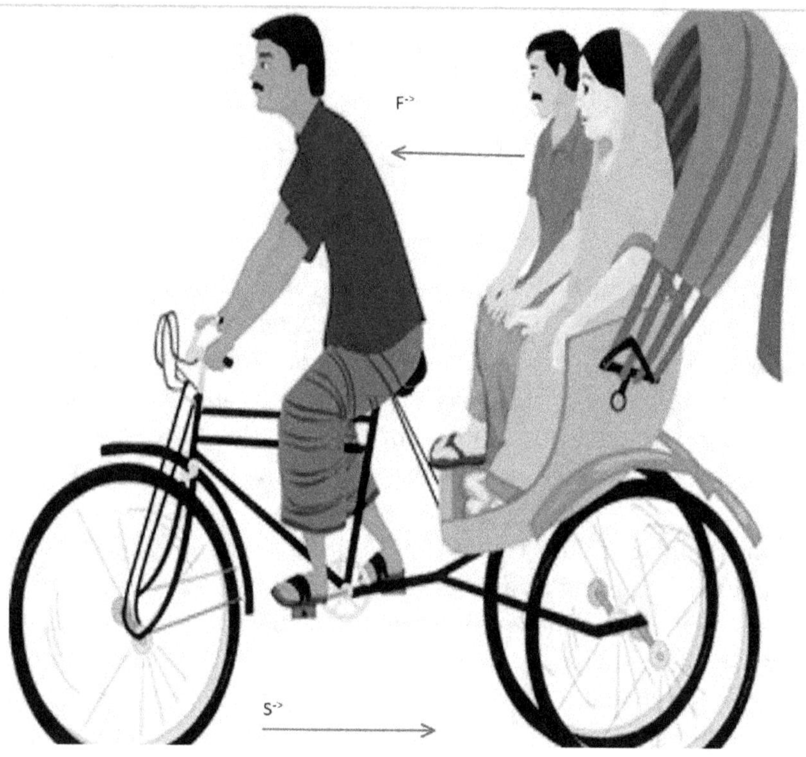

Fig.1 shows the event given in the case. '->' is used as symbol of the vector quantity and F and S are vectors.

Consider another case where an object is at rest on your house and you fly from from earth and reach any space just near to earth and you have the facility to see your home from there . Let your frame be S' and your home's(earth's frame) be S frame. You will see that in your home the object is static but from the space object the earth moving, but at very slow rate which means a very slow acceleration. You observe that the object is at rest , but if you consider the object and the earth 's frame is the same, then you observe that the body is moving but at very low acceleration , which means a very low velocity. So, by assuming this, we can state that the earth's frame is an inertial frame uptill a certain extent. Otherwise earth is also considered as non-inertial in some cases. So in this case, the normal reaction(see chapter 4) is not perfectly equal to the gravitational pull (see chapter 3) because the earth is moving, but the acceleration is almost negligible, and so the net force is also considered as zero approximately. So, here we can consider the First law of Newton is also valid here. See Fig.2 .

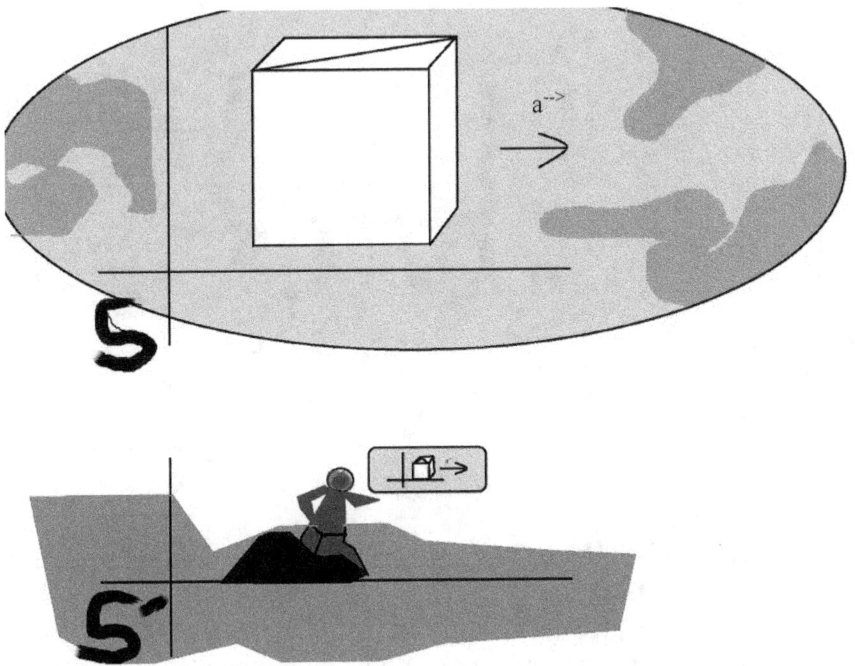

Fig. 2 the event is described above.

2nd LAW OF MOTION

The Acceleration of a Particle in an inertial frame is given by the vector sum of all the force acting on the body diveded by the mass of the body. Or, in symbols we can say it as net acceleration=net Force applied to body/the mass of the body. Thus frome we get the formula F=ma , where F is the net force , m is the mass and the a is the net acceleration acting on the body.

Consider a case where there a car is moving on the road, the friction constant on the Road is μ and so the Frictional force exerted is 'F2=μH' and the other forces like Normal reaction'H', Gravitational Force 'U' and the force exerted on the by the Engine, or we can say that is the external force applied 'F1' on the car. As in Fig . 4, we can see there are four forces acting on it, which are Normal reaction 'H', Gravitational Force 'U' , the force exerted on the vehicle by the Engine'F1 and the Frictional Force 'F2=μH' so the force exerted by each of the tyre can be calculated by vector sum of U,H,F1 and F2, so if the mass of the body is 'm' then the acceleration of the body can be calculated by the net force/ mass of the car. and the Free body Diagram is : Fig. 3

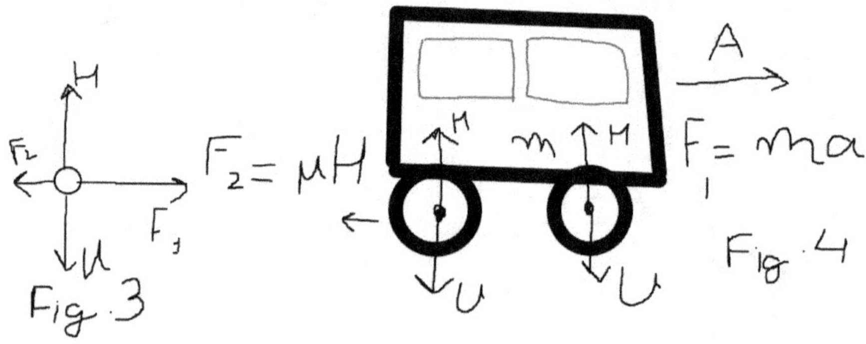

Fig. 3 & Fig. 4

WORKING WITH THE LAWS OF MOTION: 1st LAW OF MOTION AND 2nd LAW OF MOTION

The laws of Newton give us the information about the particular object's motion. Which way we are moving? Why we are moving ? In which direction we are moving? etc. questions are all answered using mostly these two laws. However, we should also remember and think about the system . Suppose that there is a mass m1, and m2 , and they are in contact to each other, So we consider m1 and m2 as system and we can add their masses, just like: (m1+m2). However, we should clear our view about the the forces acting on m1 and m2 , which depends on the direction of their motion, or more precisely the direction of their acceleration. Now after describing the forces acting on the body and their direction on which they are acting on the body we can draw the free body diagram as shown in Fig.4. Now, considering an example of an object which we can assume or imagine as that a body of mass 'm' is taking a flight at an angle θ from the ground.So lets see its representation in Fig.5 and Fig.6.

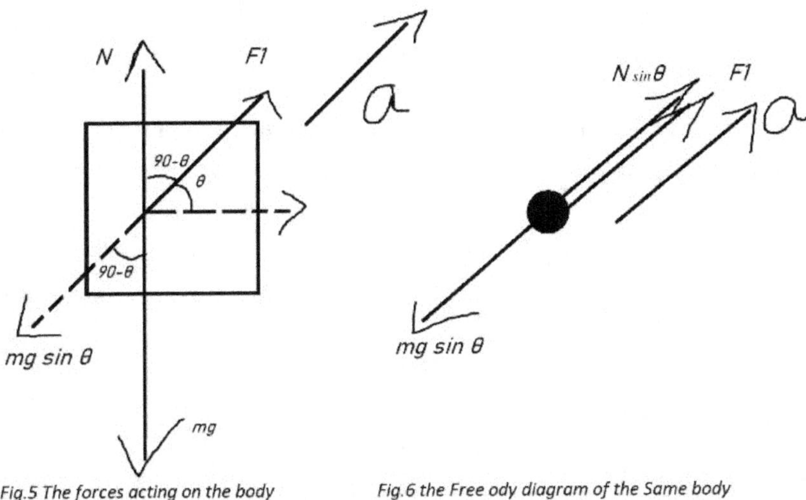

Fig.5 The forces acting on the body   Fig.6 the Free ody diagram of the Same body

Fig.5 and Fig.6 ; Free body*

Now, after mentioning this we just have to apply our logic and frame the equation according to the axis or components of the axes in which it's likely to move.For eg- here in Figs. 5&6 we have the equation of

=>F net= m*a

=>(F1+N sinθ)-mg sinθ)= m a

=>[(F1+(N-mg) sin θ]/m= a

Or,

a = [(F1+(N-mg) sin θ]/m

So we get the acceleration through this process, at first we do the vector sum of the forces by assuring the components of the forces acting on the body, and we then obtain the net Force acting on that particular body and divide it by the mass of the body to obtain the velocity.

3rd LAW OF MOTION

The third law of motion is very crucial to understand. It states that the action and reaction forces are equal and opposite to each other, since they act on opposite direction rather acting on the same direction. In other words , every action has an equal and opposite reaction. This means that the force you will applied on the object will again react on you in the opposite direction with respect to the direction in which you exerted the force. So, we say that the two forces add upto zero if the object is rest. So, considering

F1 and F2 the forces we say that F1+F2=0 (by doing vector sum of F1 and F2). So we can also say that F1 = -F2. But if the object is in a motion, then the object is considered to have velocity and so an acceleration is acting on it and so a force is also acting on it, as first law of motion says us. Hence we then say that the net force acting on it is equal to ma, or -ma , if the motion is towards the negative direction of the axes: x', y', z' .

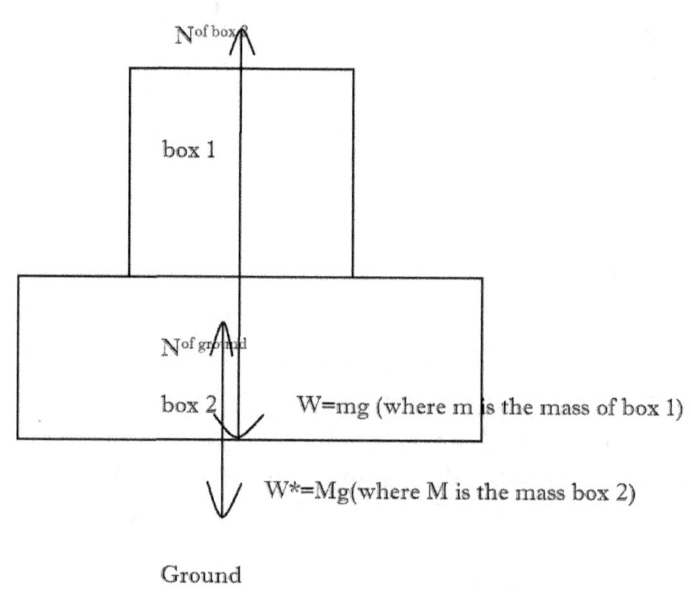

Fig. 7 Showing an example

Consider an example of Fig. 7, where we see two boxes , box 1 and box 2 wher we see the action and reaction forces of the boxes. Here is the chart for these action and reaction forces :

System	Action Force	Reaction Force
Box 1(to be mentioned about the forces acting on box 2 and by box 2 on box 1)	Weight[W=mg(on box 2)]	Normal reaction(applied by box 2 on box 1)
Box 2(to be mentioned about the forces acting on ground and by ground on box 2)	Weight[W=mg(on Ground)]	Normal reaction(applied by ground on box 2)

Here weight applied by the box 2 should have been W*

INERTIA

Inertia is nothing but the tendency of an object to not move , if at rest, or to not stop and be at rest, if in the state of motion or even maintaining a direction instead of changing it when a force is applied.However, the inertia of a body depends on the mass of the body and so mass is the measure of inertia of a body. For eg. if we consider two particles one of lesser mass than other then if we apply the same forces on them , then the one less heavier will move more fast, or will get accelerated more, rather than that of the heavier particle. This state of disallowing to accelerate more is known as the sate of **Inertia**. There are three types of Inertia:

i) Inertia of Rest : The tendency of a body to continue its state of rest, despite being applied Force.

For eg. - You cannot move a train by simply using your hands, you will need more force to do that.

ii) Inertia of Motion : The tendency of a body to continue its state of motion, despite being applied Force.

For eg. - You cannot stop a moving car by simply using your muscular force.

iii) Inertia of Direction : The tendency of a body to continue its direction of motion, despite being applied Force.

For eg. - You cannot change the direction of the movement of a big rock moving in one direction by simply using your muscular force.

EQUILIBRIUM

The state of equilibrium means that state of position of the object where the net force acting on the object is zero and the object is at rest. However we sometimes see some motionor precisely positions from where you disturb the object and the object comes at rest even after disturbing it and also sometimes if disturbed starts moving, and even some it changes position and then comes to rest. So due to this we have thre states of equilibrium, they are:

1. **Stable equilibrium:** It is the state of the body where on disturbing the body also the body comes at rest at the same position. For example , see that the ball, even if disturbed comes at the same position at rest in Fig. 8 (I).

2. **Unstable equilibrium:** It is the state of the body where on disturbing the body , the body doesn't come at rest at the same position, resulting into a disturbance in its position as well as state of inertia of rest of the body,

and thus starts moving. For example , see that the ball, even if disturbed comes at the same position at rest. See Fig. 8 (II).

3. **Neutral equillibrium:** It is the state of the body where on disturbing the body, the body changes its state of inertia of rest and after some time it comes again to is state of rest but not in the same position. For example, see Fig. 8 (III)

Fig.8 Showing the different states of equilibrium in I, II and III

CHAPTER THREE

Types of Motion

Linear Motion

When a body moves in a straight path , that motion is called as <u>linear motion</u>. The car you see in a straight road with no traffic on the road , moves in linear motion .In a linear motion we can easily determine what will be the equation of that particular instant, for a path say AB, we put a point C and we tell that uptill that point the body will undergo the force of F1 and then from there it will undergo another force of F2 will be acting on it on the same direction in which F1 is acting. We get the results as that the net force acting on the body can be obtained by simply add F1 and F2. Thus this tells us that calculating the quanitities like force, acceleration, work etc. becomes easy in this types of motion. By applying the the postulates of Special Theory of relativity, can help us to get the accurate values of the quantities required very easily. But, In our everyday life we mostly face various types of motion other than that of the linear motion. So this shows that we cannot apply linear motion to every part of our life, but for the sake of simplicity and for grasping the concepts we learn first the linear one. the linear motion has been discussed in Chapter 1 and 2.

Circular Motion

Have you ever seen the wheel of a car? I guess your response to be a yes. Have you seen them rotating? When they rotate, they move forwards. This causes when they move circularly as they are circular in size. Keeping these aside, we observe that the tyre rotates , which can be depicted by this Fig. 1:

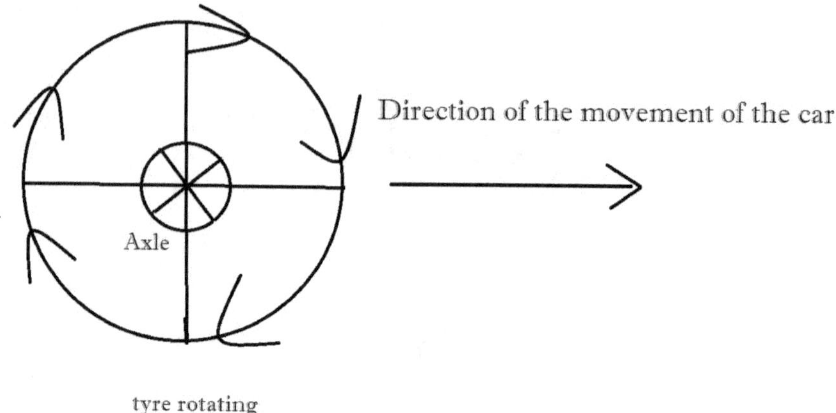

Fig. 1

In this Figure 1, we can see the axle around which there are arrows, these arrows depict the way the tyre is moving, now, again imagine yourself, holding a string that has a rock tied to one of its end. Rotate it. After seeing that motion we find that the motion can be represented just like the one in Fig.1. So, we say that the movement of a body in a circular or elliptical pathway , provided that its seen from a frame of reference, is called a circular motion. In the circular motion we get the angular variables like:

i)'θ'-Angular Displacement

Its the angle displaced a particle the circumference of the circular path in a circular motion. Its formula is:

$\theta = s/r$,where s is the arc length, r is the radius of the path and θ is the angular displacement.

ii)'ω'-Angular Velocity

Its the Rate of angular displacement of the particle per unit time. Its formula is:

$\omega = \theta/t$, where the θ is the angular displacement, t is the time and ω is the angular velocity.

Also,

as, $v = s/t$ and $\theta = s/r$

Putting s = θ r in v = s/t

we get,

=> v = θ r /t

=> v = r ω [∵ ω=θ/t]

ω = v/r...............another equation for angular velocity stating that angular velocity is the tangential velocity (linear velocity) per unit radii considered.

iii) 'α'- Angular Acceleraton

Its the Rate of the change of Angular Velocity is known a Angular Acceleration. Its Formula:

α=Δω/Δt , where α is angular acceleration, Δω is the change in angular velocity and Δt is the change in time.

iv)'τ'- Torque

Its the Force needed to move an object along a circular path or to rotate it. Its formula is:

τ=|r||F|sinθ, where r is the perpendicular length from the axis to the object, F is the force applied, and θ is the angle at which the force is applied.

v) 'L'- Angular Momentum

Angular momentum is nothing but the momentum of the particle in a rotational motion. Its Formula is :

$$\vec{L} = \vec{r} \times \vec{p} = \vec{r} \times (m\vec{v}) = m(\vec{r} \times \vec{v})$$

vi)'I'-Moment of Inertia

It ia a quantity that resists the angular acceleration and shows the tendency of the body to move in a circular motion. Its the sum of the products of masses of the particle and the radius squared, individually. Its formula is derived like this:

$$\Rightarrow F = m\vec{a}$$

$$\Rightarrow \vec{F}\vec{r} = m\vec{a}\vec{r}$$

$$\Rightarrow \vec{\tau} = m\vec{a}\vec{r}{}^{\wedge}2 \quad \_[\text{using } \vec{\tau} \equiv \vec{r} \times \vec{F}, \vec{a} = \vec{r} \times \vec{\alpha}]$$

$$\Rightarrow \vec{\tau} = m(\vec{r})^2\vec{\alpha}$$

If we compare the equation obtained of torque with the equaton of linear force, we get to know that the moment of Inertia is a mass of the body which resists the force applied to it(the torque applied to it). It is just like the inertia of rest in a linear motion.

So, moment of inertia is expressed as:

I = mr^2...................where I is the moment of inertia , m is the mass of the object and r is the radius of the orbit in which the object is circular motion.

Projectile Motion

Its the motion of a particle under the influence of gravity is calleed as projectile motion. It includes the examples of the ball thrown at a height , and also when done the same with a stone , we can also observe it in the ascending or descending of a object like Plane, or helicopters etc. In Fig.2 you can get a clearer idea about the projectile motion.

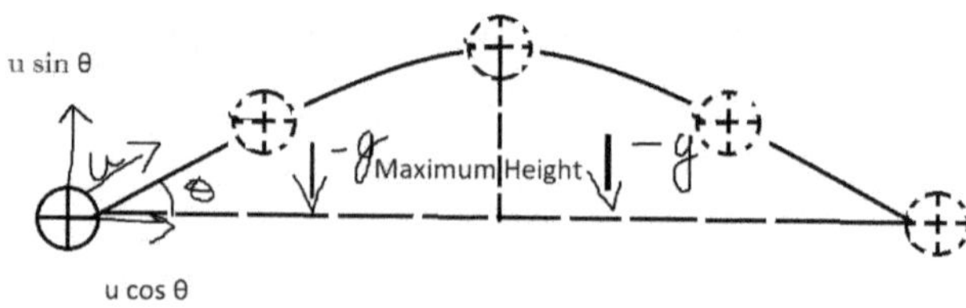

Fig . 2 The projectile motion of a ball thrown.

Here in Fig. 2 we get to see many terms. Those are defined in the following statements:

So, in a projectile motion the ball moves in u velocity to a maximum height 'H' , the ball's velocity component in the y direction i.e. u sinθ, at the point of the maximum height becomes zero, but one thing to observe is that the velocity component in the x direction does not change as in the x direction there is no accelertaion acting, hence the velocity of the ball changes when the ball rises with a deceleration, reaches the maximum height and start accelerating in the y' direction with a acceleration of +g, other when the ball just was moving upwards and reached the point of maximum height, the ball's velocity in the y direction was getting de-accelerated due to the influence of -g. this motion happenned with the body in time 't'. We consider that the place where the ball is thrown, there is no air friction.

So the time of flight is :

Considering only the motion in y axis;

We get,

$S=0$

$u=u \sin\theta$

$t=t$ [∵ the same time interval is being observed with the changes in velocity component of the body in the y axis as well as the full motion of the body, here, the ball.]

$a=-g$

using the second equation of motion , we get,

$=>0=(u \sin\theta)t+(-gt^2)/2$

$=>(gt^2)/2 = (u \sin\theta)t$

$=>gt=2 u \sin\theta$

$=>t=(2 u \sin\theta)/g$

Now, if we want to find the maximum height the ball will reach, The expression for the maximum height covered is like this :

$S=H$

$u=u \sin\theta$

$v=0$

$a=-g$

so by using third equation of the motion,

we get,

$=>(0)^2=(u^2)(\sin\theta)^2 +(-2gH)$

=>2gH=(u^2)(sin θ)^2

=>H=[(u^2)(sin θ)^2]/2g

Now, we find the formula of the displacement of the ball along the x axis , which we name as 'R':

S=R

u=u cos θ

t=t=[2 u sin θ]/g

a=0 [∵ there is no force acting in the x axis, and thus no acceleration acting in the x axis according to Newton's first law]

so by using the second equation of motion, we get,

=>R=[{u cosθ}*{2 u sinθ}]/g+[(0)*{(2 u sinθ)/g}^2]/2

=>R=(u^2)(2 sinθ cosθ)/g

=>R=(u^2)(sin2θ)/g............. [using the trigonometric identity: 2 sinθ cosθ = sin2θ]

The two highlighted equations can be used .

The equation of trajectory of the projectile can be found by the following:

t=[x/ucosθ]

u=usinθ

a=-g

therefore,

by using the third equation of motion ,

we get,

y=u sinθ(x/ucosθ)-[g(x/ucosθ)^2]/2

=>y=x tanθ - [(gx^2)/2(u^2)(cosθ)^2]

=>y=x   tanθ   -   [(gx^2)(sinθ)/2(u^2)((cosθ)^2)   (sinθ)]
...............*[multiplying sin θ to both denominator and numerator in the second in the LHS of the equation]*

=>y=x tanθ - [(gx^2)(tanθ)/(u^2)(sin2θ)] ....[∵ 2sinθcosθ=sin2θ]

=>y=x tanθ[1-x/R] ....[∵ u^2[sin2θ]/g =R]

So, as we can see, the above two highlighted equations may be used for calculating the trajectory of the projectile .

CHAPTER FOUR

The Types of Forces

According to the third law of newton the Forces are dividing into TWO TYPES:

1. **Action Forces**

Consider the case of storm, and assume yourself that you are at asafe place and the wind is blowing very in the x direction and a tree is under its influence. You will find that the tree is a bit leaned than its actual position. why this happens so? lets explore and analyse it. See Fig. 1

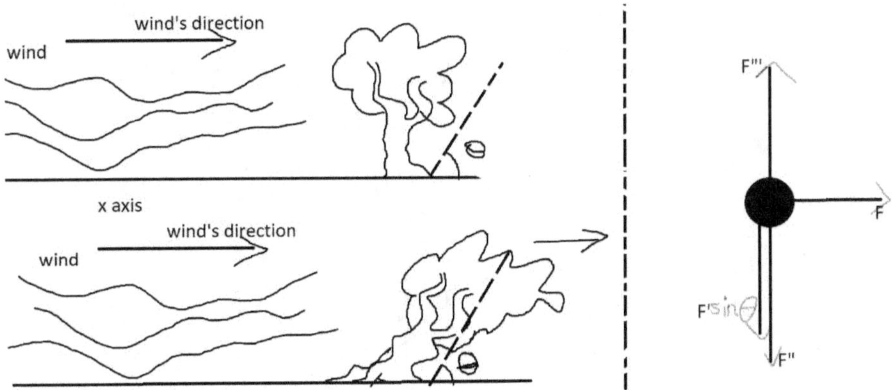

Fig.1 The storm

So as in Fig. 1, we see that the tree has leaned to an angle θ , so here the Forces of the wind and that of the Normal reaction(F and F''' respectively) and the forces immediately opposing it are the Gravitational Force and that of the Tree Roots(F'' and F' sin θ). And because of the Resultant action forces of the wind and normal reaction it becomes leaned .

So , we can say that, the forces which acts on the body at first and then after that, the forces of reaction forces acts on the body are called as *Action Forces*.

2.Reaction Forces

Suppose the case of a pulley which has a chain attached. The chain is also attached to a heavy mass(just like a 10-12 kg block), Fix an axle to the pulley so that the pulley can move. Also make sure that the chain is strong enough to do the feat. Attach a paddle strongly to the side of the on one of its opposite faces. The setup should look like in the Fig.2.

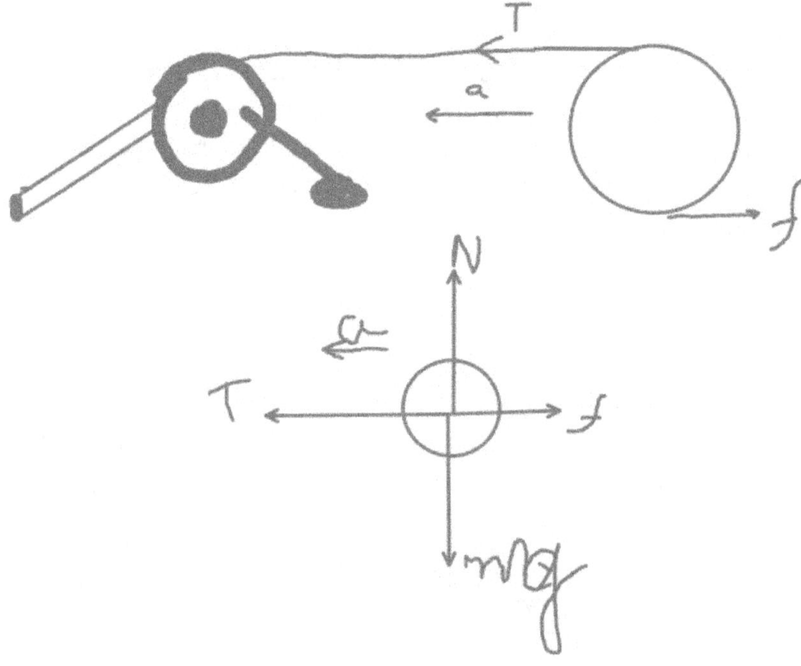

Fig.2

Thus, we see that the Normal Reaction is the reaction force that is acting on the object is the same as The Gravitational Force, this ensures that there is no movement in the y axis, but on the other hand there is the frictional Force 'f' with a friction coeffecient 'μ', which opposes the motion of the object, and has a tendency of stopping the object, this is also a reaction force, but there is also the force which is applied by the chain on the object i.e. T , but there is motion, as in Fig.2 its stated that T>f, there is a net acceleration.

So, the forces which react when any force(s) is exerted on body are called as the *Reaction Forces*.

Note: When a body is in motion then either the action force or the reaction force may be greater.

Forces can also be divided according to their strength. On that basis it has three divisions:

- **Gravitational Force**- The natural phenomenon in which there is a kind of force exerted by a celestial body on the other celestial or non celestial is called **Gravitational Force**.The acceleration due to gravity in earth is **9.8m/s^2** .They are often regarded as waves . In Quantum Theory, the gravity is hypothesised to be the force exerted by particles named as *gravitons*. Its speed is same as that of Light.
- **Electromagnetic Force**- The force exerted by the particles that are charged electrically, to each other is called as electromagnetic force. Many types of force like that of Tension, Normal reaction, Elasticity, Friction etc. are also types of Electromagnetic forces.

1. In Normal Reaction the charged particles exerts force on the object in contact to it, that's why in mars the astronauts walk like they are flying because the same normal reaction, which previously applied against the earth's gravity, and as moon's is lesser that that of earth, the astronauts float.
2. Tension on the other hand shows us the force of attraction between the atoms, that's why a silk thread is stronger than that of a cotton thread.
3. More likely in Elasticity, the particle come together due to their attraction between them, after the deformation force which is externally applied just like the streching and converging of a rubber band.
4. Friction is based on the flow of electro-static charges. It also creates a heating, on the surface as well as on the object experiencing it. the force is cause due to the attraction of chardged particles and thus cause damping of the movement of the particle in motion.

- **Nuclear Force**-The forces applied by the nucleons on each other in the nucleus. The nuclear force is way stronger than any of the forces. But the problem is, that they act in incredibly short distances which are often in femtometer(fm). They're classified into two types :

1. <u>Strong Nuclear Force</u>: This force acts between the protons and the neutron(the quarks), being responsible for the binding of the nucleus.Its the Strongest force.It acts in the quarks and gluons.
2. <u>Weak Nuclear Forces</u>:This force is responsible for the radioactive decays, like beta decay, where it was first discovered. it acts in the leptons and quarks

Fundamental Force Particles

Force	Particles Experiencing	Force Carrier Particle	Range	Relative Strength*
Gravity acts between objects with mass	all particles with mass	graviton (not yet observed)	infinity	much weaker
Weak Force governs particle decay	quarks and leptons	W^+, W^-, Z^0 (W and Z)	short range	
Electromagnetism acts between electrically charged particles	electrically charged	γ (photon)	infinity	
Strong Force** binds quarks together	quarks and gluons	g (gluon)	short range	much stronger

Fig.3 shows you the comparison table of the four fundamental forces.

We can even classify them into other sections based on different criteria: Based on the criteria that the Fnet i.e. net force adds upto zero or not:

- Balanced force: When two equal and opposite forces acts on a body, such that they do not change the state of rest or of uniform motion of the body then the forces are said to be balanced force. Balanced forces cause the deformation of a body.

- Unbalanced force: When two unequal and opposite forces acts on a body, such that they change the state of rest or of uniform motion of the body then the forces are said to be unbalanced forces. Unbalanced forces cause the motion of a body.

Based on the criteria of where the force acts:

- Contact forces The forces acting between the bodies, when they are physically in contact are called contact forces. E.g.: Frictional force, Normal reaction, Tension in a string and force acting between two bodies when they collide.
- Non – contact forces: The forces acting between two bodies, when they are physically not in contact are called non – contact forces. E.g.: Gravitational force, Electrostatic force and Magnetic force.

CHAPTER FIVE

Pseudo Forces

Consider an event where you are observing a particle in S' frame which is accelerated by a' acceleration, with respect to your inertial frame S. The acceleration of the particle with respect to S frame is a" and with respect S' Frame its acceleration is A. See Fig. 1.

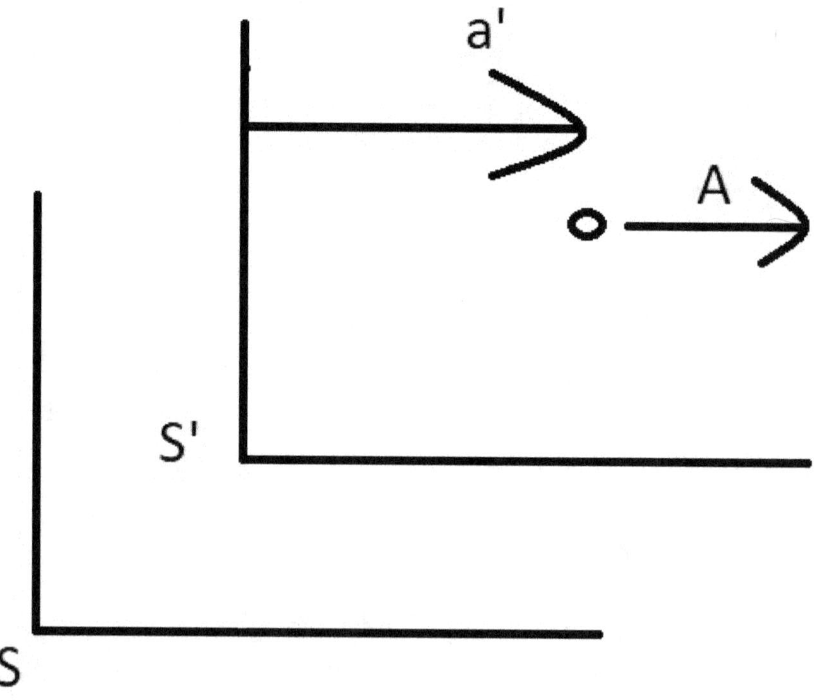

Fig. 1 The event

So since S' is translating *with respect to* S, so we can say that,

x'=x-vt, where x is the total distance and vt is the extra distance covered by the frame S' after covering x'=x, then we can double differentiate them with respect to dt, so ,

d/dt(dx'/dt) = d/dt(dx/dt)-d(vt)/dt

=>a"(a of the particle on x')= A(a of the particle on x) - a'(a of the frame S' with respect to S), [here a means acceleration.]

Now if we multiply the mass 'm' of the particle then we get,

=>ma"= mA-ma'

=>F'=F-F" [here F' is the force exerted on the particle in S' Frame , F is thge force observed from S frame , but F" is the Pseudo Force]

So we can say that, *Pseudo Forces* are the imaginary forces , which are used to make the first law and second law of Newton valid in the non-inertial frame. It only acts in the non inertial frames of reference and its formula is F=-ma, which indicates that it acts in the opposite direction of an acceleration applied(a) in the non inertial frames. They are also named as *Inertial Forces*.

Part-2 Heat and Temperature

Chapters:-

6) Heat and Temperature

7)Thermal Expansion

8)Calorimetry:-

- Specific heat capacity & heat capacity
- Specific latent heat capacity & latent heat capacity

9)Heat Transfer:

- Conduction
- Convection
- Radiation

CHAPTER SIX

Heat and Temperature

Heat and Temperature

Heat is a *Form of Energy*. It can never ever be destructed neither be created, As *The law of Conservation of Energy* says us. But It can be transferred from one body to another in any medium. Anyways, Heat itself is not sufficient to understand it , we also need to understand what is *Temperature*. Its the measure of the hotness and the coldness of a body. In other words, we can say that temperature tells us about how much heat is applied on the body, how much heat is absorbed, how much heat is emitted by the body, etc. Heat's SI unit is Joule(J) and that of temperature is Kelvin(K) . So, we can also say that Heat is Non mechanical work done by a body, or more precisely , by its molecules. As we can see that heat has the same unit as mechanical work has, but anyways they are not the same.

Transfer of Heat only happens when there is a temperature difference in the body. This creates an imbalance in the body temperature at both the sides(considering heat is applied to both the sides, i.e A and B). The molecules at the A side will vibrate more than that of B side's molecules(considering that the temperature of A side is greater than that of B side) because they will convert the heat energy absorbed by them into Kinetic Energy(The energy responsible for the movement of the body) , this will later cause into the passing of vibrations from one molecule to the other, one by one, as it also creates a potential difference in between the ends A and B. Hence the direction of the heat flow is from A to B. So this is how the heat energy is spread. There are many other methods too, like Radiation & Convection which we shall study in chapter 9.

But by this thought we should understand that temperature can also be defined as *the average energy of each molecules.*

Let us consider an example of a cuboidal box, Ther are two ends of it A & B. The end A is heated, so the temperature at A becomes T' and that at B is T.

So when you touch a place on that cuboid nearer to A you get to feel a high temperature, and as you move far away from the end A , you experience lesser and lesser temperature , as you move towards B. But after some time, you observe a temperature difference at every point . the temperature you experienced earlier has now increased. This happens because of the flow of the *Heat Energy*. See Fig.1,

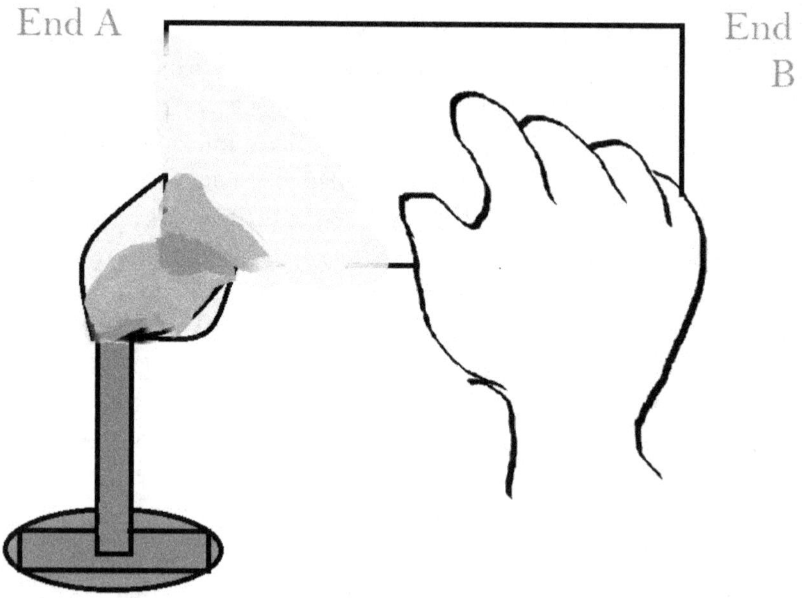

Fig.1 Showing the example

<u>Thermometry, and measurements of temperature scales</u>

The Branch which deals with the measuring of Temperature is called as **Thermometry.**

For the measuring of temperature, we consider the temperature of *solidification point* of a substance and the *vaporising point* of the same.

Water	Solidification point	Vaporising point	
	0°C	100°C	Temperature in celsius
	32°F	212°F	Temperature in Fahrenheit

table to show the temperatures of water at different points i.e the ice point and the steam point

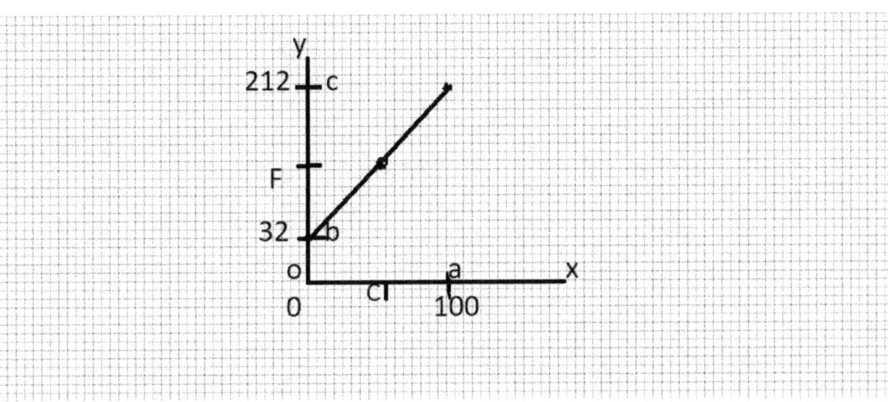

A graph to show the comparison of temperature in Celsius and temperature in Fahrenheit

Since its a linear graph,
the slope of the graph uptill(C,F)= The slope of the graph uptill (a,c)
=>[(F-32)/(C-0)]=[(212-32)/(100-0)]
=>[(F-32)/C]=180/100
=>(F-32)/C=9/5
Now from here we get two values:
one for Fahhrenheit to Celsius i.e. (5(F-32)/9) =C
And,
Celsius to Fahrenheit i.e. (9C/5)+32=F.
So through this way we can compare the temperatures of different scales. Summarizing it, the Steps to do it are:

1. Make a table of the ice point(temperature at which the water becomes ice according to the scale given to convert to another scale) and the steam point(temperature at which water stasrts vaporizing according to the scale gien to convert to another scale) of water or any other substance.

2. Plot a graph of it.

3. Mark any point on the graph between the two points given.

4. Equate the slopes under the points you marked now and the points that you marked earlier.

5. You get the equation to solve for the values for different scales.

CHAPTER SEVEN

Thermal Expansion

When the molecules of matter get exposed to heat, they get excited. This excitation causes them to vibrate. They vibrate and vibrate as they get more and more supply of heat energy. Thus this causes them to expand. They surely do get pulled by the force attraction but slowly when the kinetic energy is sufficient to break through the force of attraction, opposing their motion outwards, this causes the molecules to gain spaces between them, Thus they *Expand.* We can consider them as a system of spring attached to four balls at the corner, which when pulled from sides EXPANDS. Here we are just considering 4 molecules of something and are observing their behaviour See Fig. 1.

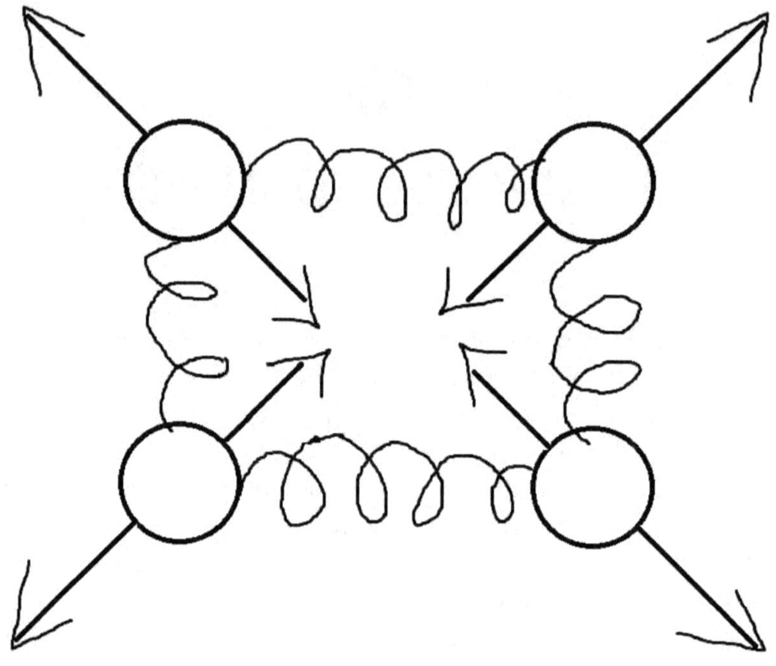

Fig. 1 Representation of the system

Now let's see this graph below,

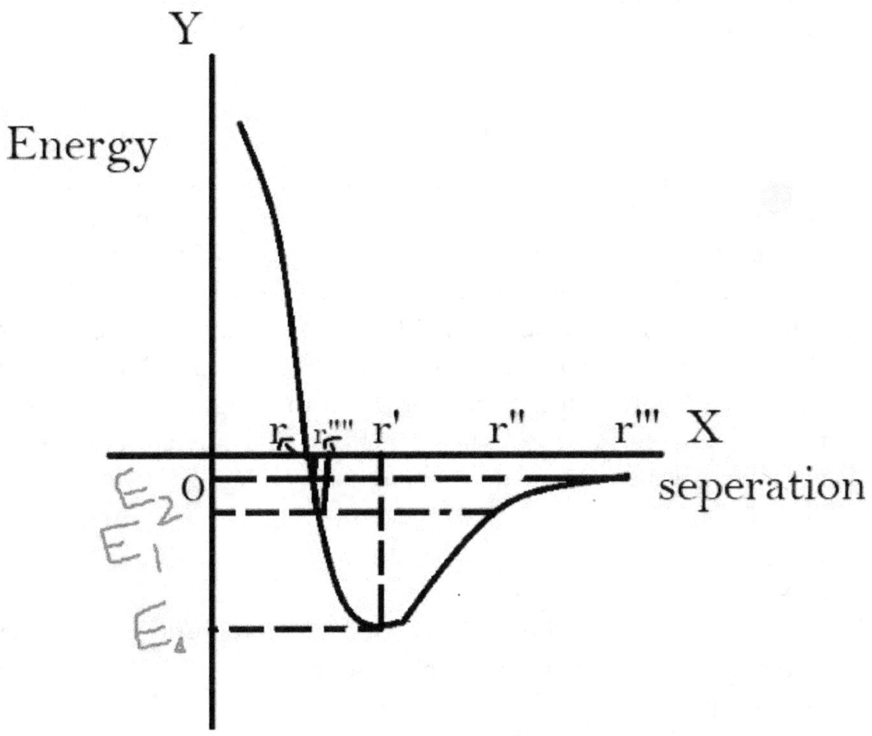

This graph of Energy(E) v/s the Seperation(r) of the molecules. This shows us that , as the molecules gain space the molecules loose potential energy, because from the position r' in the graph, the more we heat the molecules, more the molecular seperation increases between the molecules. Here, we can also observe that the length of the line between the points r and r' as well as the line between the points r"" and r' is smaller than that of the line between the points r' and r''' as well as r" and r' respectively at the energy levels E1 and E2 respectively. This implies that there is a to and fro motion in the molecules which causes them to come backwards and then again go forwards, but as we observed that the length of the line to the right of the r' point is greater than that of the length of the lines to the left of r' point, so, the net resultant is expansion of the molecules. [read every ' as dash, like r' as--->r dash]

Note: Read every objects with ' as [the object]' -> [the object] dash, like T' as T dash. And while writing these symbols you have just write the variable say T, and put a dash vertically on the upper right side of T.

Types of Expansions

There are three types of Expansion , they are as follows:

- ### Linear Expansion

Linear Expansion is the expansion of an object in one dimension on applying heat. Consider a rod, where at one corner, heat is applied . Observe the 1 Dimensional rod after a considerable amount of time (like 1 or 2 hours). You will see that rod has expanded linearly by ΔL, where we consider L to be the actual length and L' to be the increased length. So, ΔL = L'-L. Now, as we can notice that ΔL is directly proportional to both L and ΔT(its the temperature difference) because if the length is more, then the change in length increases and when the change in temperature is more the change in length is also more, this implies that:

$\Delta L \propto \Delta T$

and,

$\Delta L \propto L$

so by multiplying L and ΔT on the LHS with a proportionality constant 'α' i.e. the coeffiecient of linear expansion we get ΔL,

$\Delta L = \alpha L \Delta T$

or in differential form,

$dL = \alpha L dT$

α depends on the material, because if the material absorbs more heat then it will expand more, so ΔL will be more, and if that's more, then the value of α is more. Its SI unit is 1/Kelvin(K). The coeffiecient of linear expansion can also be said as the change in length per unit temperature per unit length.It depends on the material and differs from material to material.

- ### Aerial Expansion

Apply heat on a metal sheet, you will observe that the area of the metal sheet has prominently increased after a period of time say, 1 hour or so. This is called *Aerial Expansion*. In other words it is the 2 dimensional expansion of the material on heating it. Let ΔA be the change in Area of the material, considering the final area as A' and the initial area as A. So $\Delta A = A'-A$. Let the temperature difference in the material be $\Delta T = T'-T$ where the T' term is the final Temperature and the T is initial Temperature. So we can say that $\Delta A \propto A$ because if the area is more, the change in area is also more, $\Delta A \propto \Delta T$ because more the change in temperature more is the change in Area.

Thus we can express ΔA in the form of :

$\Delta A = \beta \, A \, \Delta T$ .... where β is the coefficient of Aerial Expansion which can again be defined as the change in Area per unit time per unit Area. Its SI unit is 1/Kelvin(K). It also depends on the material and differs from material to material.

We can also get a relation between the coefficient of Linear expansion and the coefficient of Aerial expansion by the following method:

We know that ,

$\Delta A = \beta A \Delta T$

$=> \beta A \Delta T = \Delta A$

$=> \beta A dT = dA$ .... [Considering a very small change in area and in Temperature]

$=> (dA/dL)*dL = \beta A dT$ .... $[\because$ Area is L^2]

$=> (d(L\text{^}2)/dL)*dL = \beta A dT$

$=> 2L*(\alpha L dT) = \beta(L\text{^}2)dT$ .... $[\because dL = \alpha L dT]$

$=> 2\alpha = \beta$

- **Volumetric Expansion**

When Heat is provided to a 3 dimensional object , there is an expansion in the object's dimensions. Consider a sphere, which is heated , the dimensions of the sphere also gets increased, and so does the volume . Thus by this we understand that more is the change in the Volume, more the Volume of the material increases, and more is the change in Temperature , more is the change in Volume. So by considering, the change in Volume as ΔV , the change in temperature as ΔT and the Volume of the material as V, we get the expression for ΔV as:

$\Delta V = \gamma V \Delta T$, where γ is the coefficient of Volumetric Expansion. It is the change in volume per unit change temperature per unit volume. It also depends on the material and differs from material to material. It also depends on temperature prominently. Its SI unit is 1/Kelvin(K).

or in differential form as,

$dV = \gamma V dT$

we can express it in terms of α & β too, just like this:

we know,

$dV=\gamma VdT$

$=>(dV/dL) *dL =\gamma VdT$ [∵ Volume is L^3]............... (i)

$=>(3L^2)dL=\gamma(L^3)dT$

$=>(3L^2)\alpha LdT=\gamma(L^3)dT$ [∵ dL=αLdT]

$=>3\alpha=\gamma$ --> a relation between α & γ

Now, from the above relation, we can derive the relation between β & γ,

$=> 3(\beta/2) =\gamma$ .... [∵ 2α=β =>α=β/2]

$=> 3\beta/2 =\gamma$ --> a relation between β & γ

<u>**Observations based on the thermal expansion property of the body**</u>

Anomalous expansion of water

Normally we observe that an object when heated gets expanded. Much the opposite way it gets contracted when the temperature decreases. But, for that, **Water** is bit a kind of different. It expands from exactly **4 degree celsius** to **0 degree celsius**. This is anomalous, which means strange, and which breaks the law(s); since water is expanding at **4 degree celsius** rather than contracting at that temperature. This cause the increase in the volume of water because the density decreases in water due to this expansion of water. This is also the cause for ice getting freezed only at the upper layer of the water bodies in the cold countries as the layers of water of come up gets cooler, then goes down, but when the water's temperature reaches 4 degree celsius, the water inside expands but when another layer of water comes up and reaches 0 degree celsius the upper layer gets freezed into ice. Thus, because this the organisms inside the water body remains alive because the water remains in its liquid state inside and as ice on the upper surface. See the graphs below

VOLUME AND DENSITY OF WATER VS TEMPERATURE - DIAGRAM

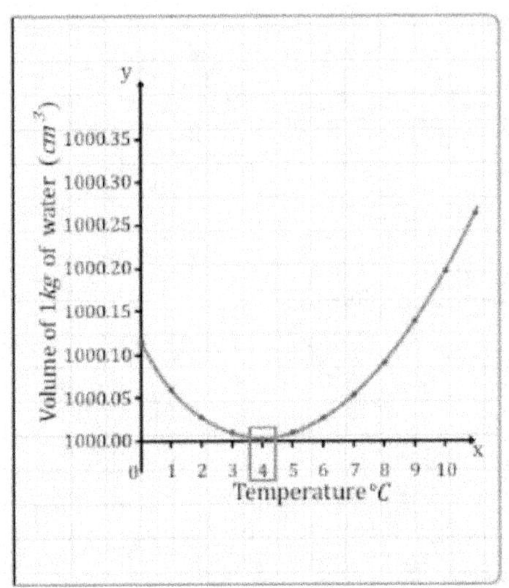

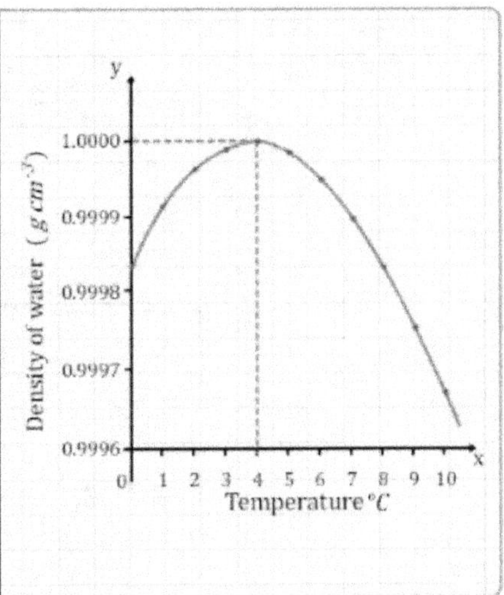

So, these are graphs, where we see the change in water with respect to volume and density as it reaches 0 degree celsius.

Note: In other materials cooling has an effect in increasing the density of it, but in water during cooling, as the water molecules gets arranged into a particular lattice (pattern); there are cavities created, becoming lighter (at 4 degree celsius) and after this stage it normally gets cooler and denser.

Bimetallic Strip

Consider two metals of identical lengths L which are stuck together very tightly. One of them has α' & the other has α which is lesser than the former. Let the metals be named as A and B, where A has α' coefficient of linear expansion which is greater than α of B. So as they are stuck together very tightly, the metal A will expand more on heating the bimetallic strip than that of metal B, because α'> α. As a result, the strip will get curved where metal A will force metal B to increase its length too as A does, but B will again resist it , and will form a concave structure. Just like in Fig . 2

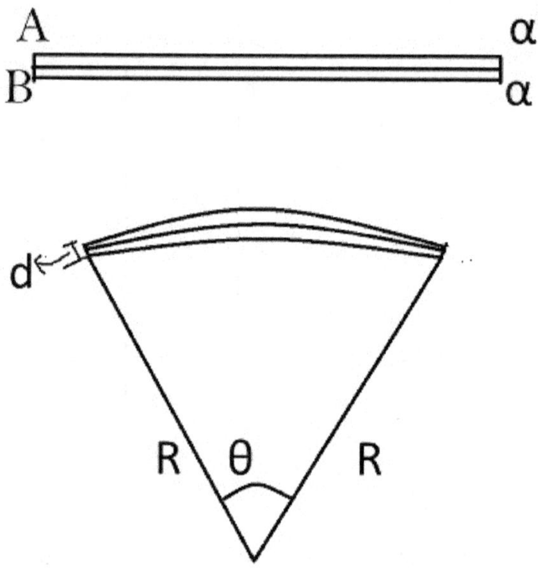

Fig.2 Showing the conditions of two bimetallic rod before and after heating

After heating the bimetallic strip, we get them curved, they make an angle θ as shown in Fig.2 and have Radius R the strip's width is d. So, we can write that :

The expanded length of A(L2a) and that of B(L2b) is ,

L2a=(R+d)θ......(i)

L2b=Rθ......(ii)

Also,

L2a=Lα'ΔT+L=L(1+α'ΔT).......(iii)

L2b=LαΔT+L=L(1+αΔT)........(iv)

equate (i) with (iii) and (ii) with (iv)

we get,

(R+d)θ=L(1+α'ΔT)..........(v)

Rθ=L(1+αΔT)...............(vi)

Do (v)/(vi)

we get,

1+d/R=(1+α'ΔT)/(1+αΔT)

=>d/R=[1+α'ΔT -1-αΔT]/1+αΔT

=>R=d(1+αΔT)/(α'-α)ΔT -----> This gives us the radius R

Defect or Fault in Metallic Scales due to temperature change

Suppose that you are having a metallic scale showing you the reading of the length of the object as G units, now as you go on heating the same scale you will ge to see that the metal scales is now showing the readings of the body to be smaller. Similarly when you cool the metallic scale more, it will contract, thus getting smaller and showing bigger readings of the same object.

Since the object has a true reading of G units initially, and after expansion it got decreased, So here the measured length we get is the actual length of the object with respect to the True Scale added by the net increase in the length of the scale. So the formula of True reading of the metal scale is :

True Reading = Measured Length - ΔL of the Scale, where ΔL = αLΔT

This was during Expansion of the material but during the Contraction of the metal scale,

we get,

True Reading = Measured Length + ΔL of the Scale, where ΔL = αLΔT

Faulty Pendulum Based Clock

Consider the Pendulum M, with the string length L, which is now heated, due to which the length of the string gets increased. Let this length be L'. So L' = L (1+αΔT)

Now, as we know that, the **Time** of a pendulum is given by $2\pi\sqrt{(L/g)}$

then we get that,

As, time(T) $\propto \sqrt{(L)}$,

So we get,

T=$2\pi\sqrt{(L/g)}$ [where T is the Time earlier, when it (M) was not heated]

T'=$2\pi\sqrt{(L'/g)}$ [where T' is the Time after, when it (M) got heated up]

So,

$T'/T = [2\pi\sqrt{(L'/g)}\,]/[2\pi\sqrt{(L/g)}]$

$=> T'/T = \sqrt{[L'/L]}$

$=> T'/T = \sqrt{\{L(1+\alpha\Delta t)/L\}}$............. $[\because L'=L(1+\alpha\Delta t)]$

$=> T'/T = \sqrt{(1+\alpha\Delta t)}$.................. [Since, when x<<1, $(1+x)^n\approx 1+nx$]

$=> T'=T(1+\alpha\Delta t/2)$

$=> T'=T+T\alpha\Delta t/2$ ----------> **For T' , or the Time after (M)got heated up, causing the string to extend**

$=> T'-T=T\alpha\Delta t/2=\Delta T$-----------> **For ΔT , or the change in Time period of after M got heated up and before.**

If the body got cooler the Δt would become negative which would cause ΔT to be negative, and will make the eqn. below:

$T'=T-T\alpha\Delta t/2$

So,

$\Delta T=-T\alpha\Delta t/2$

Note: Here, we are considering temperature as small T rather than the normal and classic capital T so that the confusion of Time period and Temperature change can be omitted.

Effect on Density of the Liquid

Suppose a liquid of mass m, volume v and of coeffiecient of volumetric expansion, 'γ'. It's now heated up, so its mass is constant, but the volume becomes v+dv and the change in temperature is dT. Now, we see that,

$\rho=m/v$-----(i)

$\rho'=m/v+dv$----(ii)

By dividing (ii)/(i),

we get,

$\rho'/\rho = v/v+dv$

$=> \rho'/\rho=v/v+v\gamma dT$

$=> \rho'/\rho=1/1+\gamma dT$

$=> \rho'/\rho=1/1+\gamma dT$.................... [Since, when x<<1, $(1+x)^n\approx 1+nx$]

$=> \rho'/\rho=1-\gamma dT$

$=> \rho'=\rho-\rho\gamma dT$ ------>The formula for the decrease/increase in density when the material is heated.

$=> \rho'-\rho=-\rho\gamma dT =\Delta\rho$ ------->The formula for the change in density of the material when heat is applied on it.

CHAPTER EIGHT

Calorimetry

Calorimetry is the study of the measurement of Heat. Through calorimetry we can know that how much heat is flowing through a material in a particular temperature difference. Calorimetry also have some constants associaled with it. Those are:

Specific heat capacity & Heat capacity

Specific Heat Capacity is the amount of heat required to increase **1 degree celsius** of **1 gram** of a substance. It is material dependent. It's SI unit is Joule(J)/Celsius(degree C) gram(g) or J/gC or even Joule(J)/Kelvin(K) gram(g) i.e J/gK .

Consider water in a saucepan, which is heated, we observe that the heat energy 'Q' is directly proportional to Mass 'm' and the change is temperature 'ΔT' because more is mass, more the heat is required and more is the heat applied, more is the change in temperature.

we get that,

$Q \propto \Delta T$

$Q \propto m$

$Q = mc\Delta T$, where m is mass, ΔT is the change in temperature and c is the specific heat capacity, which is also the proportionality constant. We should know and understand that when the specific heat capacity of a substance is higher then the heat is absorbed more by the substance and when the substance has its specific heat capacity lower, the substance gets easily heated.

Heat Capacity is the amount of heat required to increase 1 degree celsius of the substance. It is material dependent. It's SI unit is Joule(J)/Celsius(degree C) or J/C , or, Joule(J)/Kelvin(K) or J/K . It is also called Thermal Capacity.

Just from the previous equation we just takeout the part of 'mc' in $Q = mc\Delta T$, where m is mass and c is the specific heat capacity, which is also the proportionality constant and here also when the heat capacity is more the object absorbs heat more and when its less the object gets easily heated.

So we can also write ,

$Q=(mc) \Delta T$

or,

Heat energy = Heat capacity * Change in temperature

Both are *Material Dependent*.

Differences between **Heat capacity** & **Specific heat capacity** :

<u>Heat capacity</u>

1. Depends on Mass

2. Not constant for every Mass

<u>Specific heat capacity</u>

1. Does not depend on Mass

2. Constant for every Mass (i.e. 1 gram of the substance)

<u>Latent heat and Specific Latent Heat</u>

Latent word itself means Hidden. So in context to the topic of Latent heat it would mean the hidden amount of Heat. **Latent Heat** basically means the amount of heat needed to change the state of an amount of a material . During this, the temperature remains constant and the molecules of the substance obtains the heat energy and converts it into kinetic energy.

The Specific Latent heat 'L' is nothing but the amount of latent heat required (to gain or lose) to change the state of 1 gram of a material. It is specific because it specifies the amount of substance we take, it is material dependent.

For example:- when water at 0 degree celsius gets converted into ice at 0 degree celsius it releases latent heat and if we observe the reverse process, i.e. when ice at 0 degree celsius gets converted into water at 0 degree celsius, we see that the latent heat is absorbed. This also helps us to infer that *when a substance is contracting the substance is loosing Latent Heat and when its expanding the substance is gaining Latent Heat*. Its SI unit is Joule 'J'. Both are *Material Dependent*.

So,

we know that more the Latent heat is absorbed more the heat is required, so we can say that

Latent Heat$(Q)\propto$ Specific Latent heat (L)

Latent Heat$(Q)\propto$ mass(m)

therefore, we can write,

$Q = mL$

Differences between **Latent Heat & Specific Latent Heat** :

<u>Latent Heat</u>

1. Depends on Mass

2. Not constant for every Mass

3. Its the heat energy itself

<u>Specific Latent Heat</u>

1. Does not depend on Mass

2. Constant for every Mass (i.e. 1 gram of the substance)

3. Its the capacity of the material

<u>Note</u>:

1) A substance having low or high Specific Heat Capacity would heat up more or less quickly respectively and same is for Heat Capacity

2) A substance having less specific latent heat will indicate that it can change its state with the supply of very less heat or by losing very less heat and having its value more indicates that it requires more heat (to gain or lose) in order to change its state. The same is for Latent Heat.

<u>**Principle of Calorimetry**</u>

Consider a body having very high temperature. Now place another body near it having a lower temperature. After sometime, you will see that the temperature of both the bodies will be in equilibrium. It is very obvious that there would be a transfer of heat, according to this formula $Q=mc\Delta T$ where we see that the change in temperature is directly proportional to the heat energy flowing. But, another thing to observe here is that we see the temperatures equalizing (coming in equilibrium state with respect to each other). And, by that we know that the heat energy is equalized in both the bodies.

So, basically, what the Principle of Calorimetry states, is that the heat gained by the body is exactly the same as the heat losed by the body which transfers the heat to the other body(s). Hence, we understand that,

Q losed = Q gained

$\therefore$ m'c'ΔT' = mcΔT ,

Where m' is the mass, c' is the specific heat capacity and ΔT' is the temperature change of the body gaining heat[on the LHS] and on RHS m is the mass, c is the specific heat capacity and ΔT is the temperature change of the body supplying heat. Its based on the *Law of Conservation of Energy.*

CHAPTER NINE

Heat transfer

Why do we feel cold by touching ice? Why we feel hotter near fire? This all happens due to Heat transfer from substances to other substances. It is basically the transfer of heat energy from one body to another. Let us consider a situation in which a rod is heated, because of which the rod's temperature is increasing at every point as shown in Fig.1.

Let the ends of the rod be A and B , by heating A there is a temperature of 100 degree celsius and slowly it passes through the body and makes the different parts of the rod have variable temperature, here variable in the sense that, first, as shown in Fig. 1, the temperature is 90 degree celsius at a particular point on the rod, then again it becomes 100 degree celsius. This happens because the molecules do not absorb all of the heat energy supplied at once, it absorbs some amount of it and then passes some amount of it. The state of the rod(material) in which the temperature at every point keeps changing due to continuos heat flow, is the *Variable State*. When the molecules vibrate at its maximum, at the place where heat is applied; they now pass over the complete heat supplied to them to the other molecules. Now, in this state the rod's temperature remains constant, is called as *Steady State*. Carefully observe Fig.1.

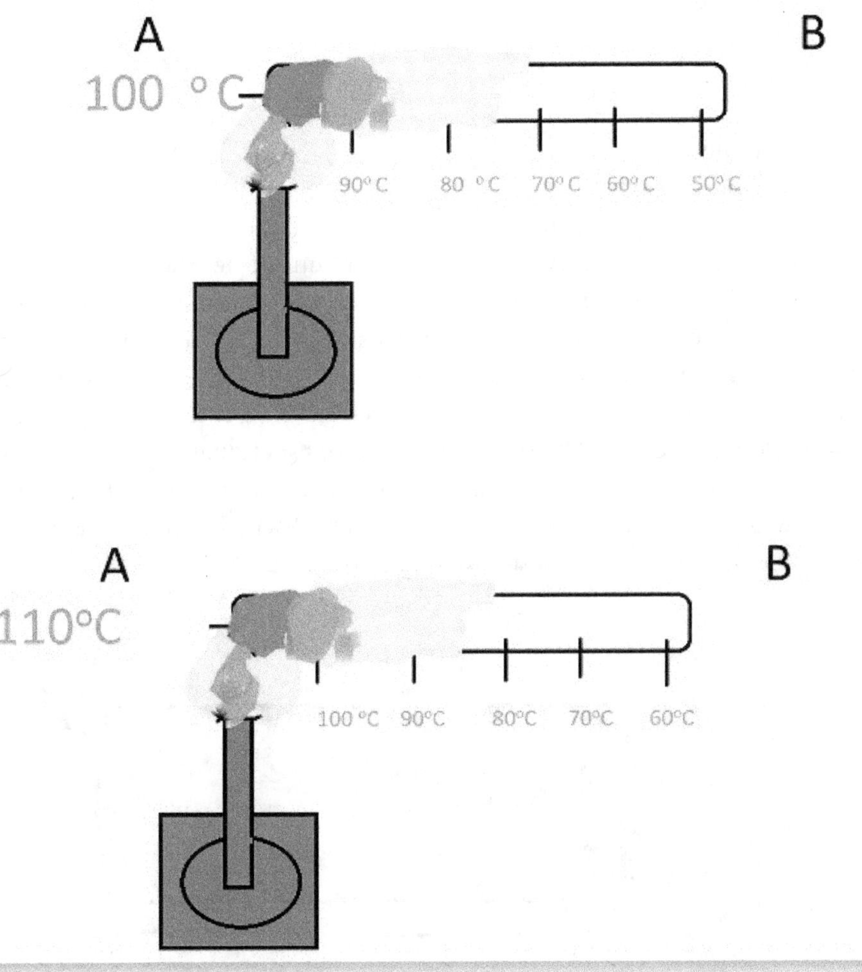

Fig.1. Showing the Rod heated and the states of the rod

For studying this chapter, we will only study steady state where we can easily calculate the Heat energy flowing through the conductor. It is also because in steady state the temperature at each point remains constant and so they (molecules supplied with heat) let the full amount of heat to pass through, without absorbing it, to the other molecules next to them .

Types of Heat Transfer

There are three types of heat transfer:

1. Conduction
2. Convection
3. Radiation

1. Conduction

1.1 Introduction

Consider a steel rod. There is burner fixed on one of its corner. It is now heated. So as it is in steady state the full amount of heat will be passed by the molecules to one another, thus ,their would be uniform flow of heat throughout the conductor rod and because of this heating by the burner there is uniform temperature difference created, whose value is constant throughout the rod. Moreover, more the time is spent, more is the heat energy flow in the rod. The rod also has a cross sectional area A which also involves in the flow of Heat, because more the cross sectional area, more is the flow of heat flow. The rod also has a length l which reduces the flow of heat energy. See Fig.2. for better visualization:

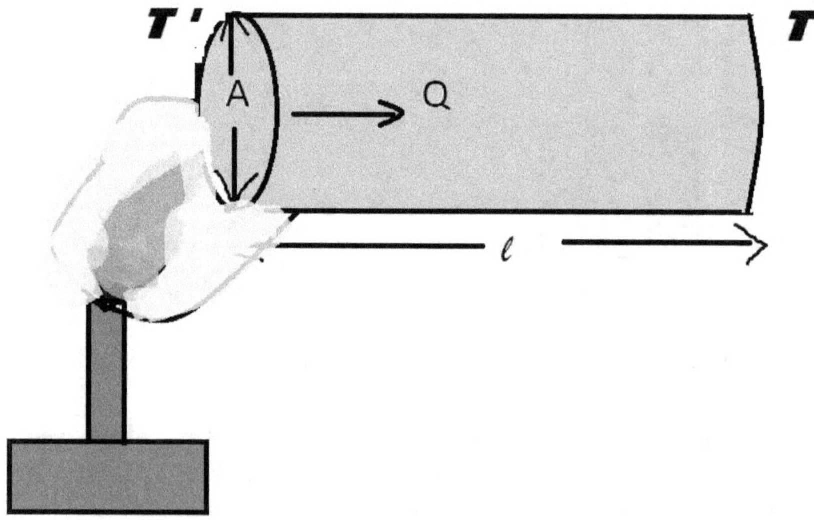

Fig. 2 the rod heated

So as we can infer that:

i) $Q \propto$ Temperature change(ΔT)..............................[where $\Delta T = T'-T$]

ii) $Q \propto$ Time (t)

iii) $Q \propto 1/$ Length (l)

iv) $Q \propto$ Area of cross section (A)

$\therefore Q = (K A \Delta T t)/l$

Or in differential form,

We can write it as:

$Q = (K A dT t)/dl$; where K is the thermal conductivity of the material, and is also a proportionality constant. it also depends on material and is different for different material.

So, we can now easily say that conduction is the flowing of Heat energy through molecular collisions, but there is no actual matter flow. It mostly happens in solids and also happens in fluids but at a very low rate because the fluids have very large molecular spaces.

1.2 Heat Current

The rate of heat flow in a body applied wit heat, is called as the *Heat Current* of the body. It also gives us the value of the heat passing per unit time in a body. It is expressed as 'H' where ,

$H=Q/t$

$=>H=((K A \Delta T t)/l)/t$

$=>H= K A \Delta T /l$

$=>H=(\Delta T)/\{l/KA\}$

or in diferential form we can write it as,

$H=dQ/dt =KAdT/dl$

As we can see that it is somewhat similar with the formula of $\Delta V=IR$, or $I=\Delta V/R$ [Ohm's law], so by comparison we can say that the terms ΔT and ΔV are similar , H and I are also similar and $R= \rho l/A$ & l/KA are also similar. Now from the comparison of these terms we get clarified about the fact that because of temperature difference, there is flow of heat, and the heat current is the heat flowing per unit time and the resistance in a condutor of heat is provided by the term l/KA which directs to our next topic i.e. :

1.3 Thermal Resistivity

It is basically the resistance provided by the material for stopping the flow of heat through it. It can also be expressed as the tendency of the object to stop the flow of heat. The material which have this property more in them are classified the insulators of heat, but the other materials which have this property less in them are called as the conductors of heat. The thermal resistivity is directly proportional to the length of the body and is inversely proportional to the thermal conductivity constant and the cross sectional area of the material . So, its expressed as :

R=l/KA, where R is the thermal resistivity

1.4 Temperature Gradient

Consider a steel strip on which you are applying heat with the help of the lighter. we observe that with the increase in length the temperature change goes on decreasing, resulting in the non-uniform distribution of the heat energy because some energy is absorbed and out of that some is transferred, causing an non uniform temperature at each cross section, just as in Fig.1. Therefore we can definetly say that length of a body depends highly on temperature of it. Hence this brings us to know about the rate of change of temperature of the body in every direction of its displacement (length) and this is Temperature Gradient. Basically, in gradient of function, we differentiate the function with respect to dx , dy and dz partially along with their respective unit vectors, it is expressed as:

Temperature Gradient = $\Delta T/\Delta l$

$\nabla T = (dTx /dx)i + (dTy /dy)j + (dTz /dz)k$

Here, we have i, j and k as the unit vectors. It is also the slope of the graph of change temperature v/s change length, see the graph below.

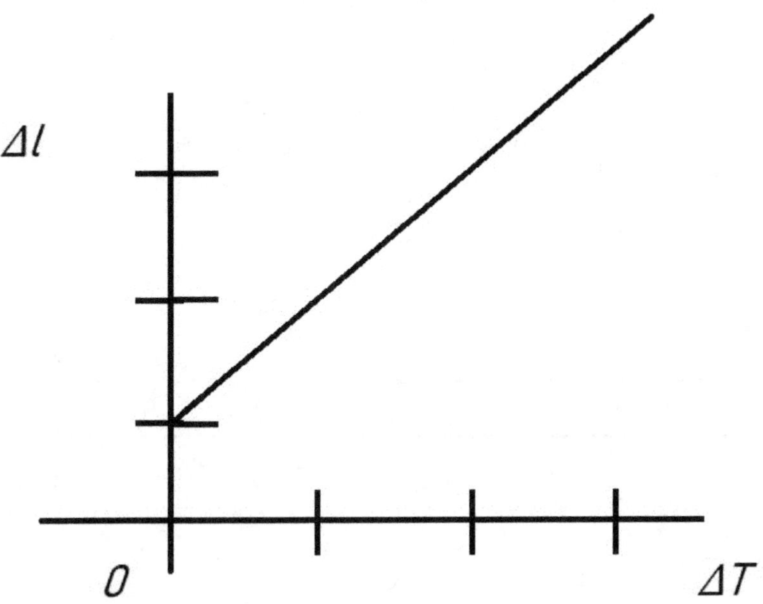

Heat & Electricity -Analogy

- Heat has heat current, which is the flow of heat per unit time, and it flows because of the difference in Temperature. Electricity has electrical current denoted by I which is the flow of Charge per unit time and it flows because of the potential difference.
- The heat current is expressed by H= $\Delta T/R$ where R is the thermal resistivity and ΔT is the temperature and H is the Heat Current. Th electrical Current represented by I=$\Delta V/R$ where ΔV is the potential difference , R is the electrical resistance and I is the electrical resistance.
- Both have Resistance which are based on the material i.e thermal resistivity and electrical resistivity, where the formulae are similar and have the same factors i.e. length and cross sectional area.

1.5 Combination of conductors & Equivalent Resistance

There are two types of combination of conductors:

1.5.i Series combination

It is the combination of the conductors where they are placed along a single line, or in other words the conductors are placed end to end, stuck together. Thus we call them to be in series because we can see that they are placed one after another. So, let us consider two different conductors which have their lengths l and l', cross sectional area A and A' thermal conductivity constant K & K', see Fig. 3.

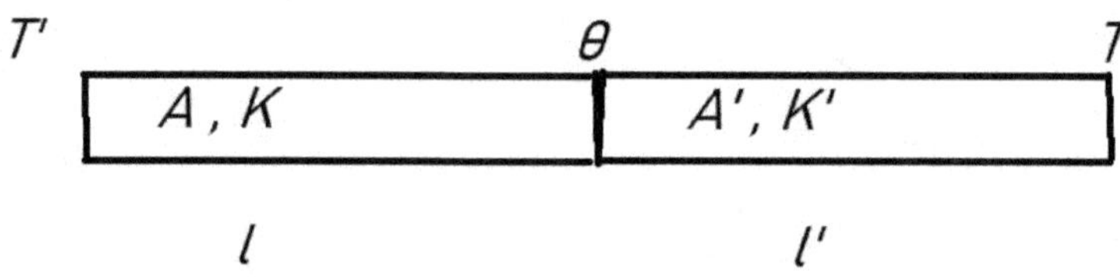

Fig. 3 showing the conductors

1.5.i.1 The Temperature of the Junction

As we can see that for the sake of heat flow there is a temperature difference, i.e. T'-T=ΔT,

So, as we also know that the conductors are in steady state and have the same heat energy flow through them so we give the equation of the heat current by this:

∵ H=H

=>KAΔT'/l=K'A'ΔT''/l'................ [here since there is an other temperature in the junction of the conductors]

=>l'KA(T'- θ)=lK'A'(θ - T)

=>l'KAT'+ lK'A'T = θ (lK'A'+l'KA)

=>θ = (l'KAT'+lK'A'T)/(lK'A'+l'KA) .... For finding the temperature at the junction

And for identical conductors,

=>θ=(lKAT'+lKAT)/(lKA+lKA)

=>θ = (T' + T) /2

We find it because they are both individual conductors who are joined in a series combination and so to see and get the results in the perspective of a single conductor we find the temperature of the junction.

1.5.i.2 Equivalent Thermal Resistance

The equivalent Thermal resistance is nothing but the net thermal resistance in the combination of conductors whether it be in parallel or in series.

So as we know that the thermal resistance of a conductor is R= l/KA, so,

R=l/KA

R'=l'/K'A'

According to this we can also write the below :

H=KAΔT'/l =ΔT'/R

=>HR= ΔT'

H'=K'A'ΔT''/l =ΔT''/R'

=>H'R'=ΔT''

$\because$ H=H'=H'',where H'' is the heat current which is equal to (T - T')/R'' , here R'' is the equivalent Thermal resistance.

H''R''=HR+H'R'

$\therefore$R''=R+R'

or,

=>R''= l/KA+l'/K'A'.................Equation for the Equivalent Thermal Resistance in a series combination

1.5.i.3 Equivalent Thermal conductivity

It is basically the heat flowing in every point per unit time per unit cross sectional area per unit change in temperature. Let's also consider the area of cross section to same here for the sake of simplicity .So from the eqn. of equivalent thermal resistance:

From the eqn. , R''=R+R'

we get,

=>(l+l')/K''A =l/KA+l'/K'A [l+l', because in series combination the length of the equivalent conductor increases]

let , (l'+l)=L

=> K'' = (LKK')/(l'K+lK').....................Eqn. for Equivalent Thermal conductivity in a series combination

1.5.ii Parallel Combination

It is the combination of the conductors where they are placed parallel to each other. Thus we call them to be in a parallel combination because we can see that they are placed parallel to each other. So, let us consider two different conductors which have same lengths l, cross sectional area A and A', and thermal conductivity constant K & K'. See Fig. 4.

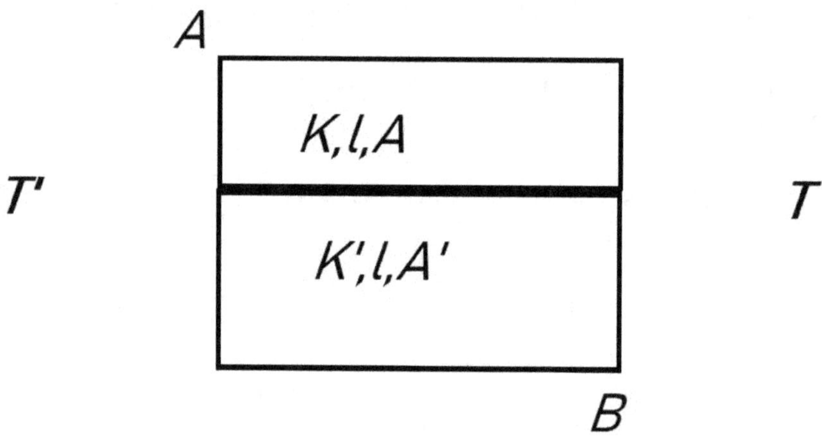

Fig.4. Showing the parallel combination

Here is no use of the temperature of the Junction because here is no Junction, the conductor are parallel here.

1.5.ii.2 Equivalent Thermal Resistance

The equivalent Thermal resistance is nothing but the net thermal resistance in the combination of conductors whether it be parallel or in series.

Now because the Heat energy flow is diverted here the Heat current in A is different as compared to B, So we can write,

H''= H + H'

=>$\Delta T/R'' = \Delta T/R + \Delta T/R'$ ....[value of ΔT is same for all the conductors in parallel combination as there is no junction in this conductor combination]

$\therefore 1/R''=1/R +1/R'$..........Equation for the Equivalent Thermal Resistance in a parallel combination

1.5.ii.3 Equivalent Thermal conductivity

It is basically the heat flowing in every point per unit time per unit cross sectional area per unit change in temperature. So from the eqn. of equivalent thermal resistance:

From the eqn. , $1/R''=1/R+1/R'$

we get,

$K''(A+A')/l=KA/l +K'A'/l$ [A+A', because in parallel circuit two or more conductors are combined parallely and hence there cross sectional area increases rather than length just like in series combination]

$=>K''=(KA+K'A')/(A+A')$.................Eqn. for Equivalent Thermal conductivity in a parallel combination

Note: In parallel circuit the cross sectional area increases so the heat current is more in parallel combination rather than that in the series combination where the length increases which decreases the heat current.

2. Convection

Convection is that mode of heat transfer where the heated material (Fluid) in contact to the heated surface moves up because of density difference and excitement and while moving up, it pushes the upper layer of material towards the surface, this is called as convection currents, which causes the convection of material (Fluid). Take the example of the water tumbler heated on a stove, or that of sight in the deserts where you see the hot air performing circular motion (convection currents), all these follow the method of convection as a mode of heat transfer.

Most certainly, it has two types,

2.i Free convection

The type of convection happening in fluids without any external influences is called as free convection. It happens because of density differences in the fluid during heating. It happens so, that the when the heating is done to the molecules of the fluid nearer to the surface of the material heated, the fluid gets heated and thus it expands, as said in chapter 7, *Thermal Expansion*; so due to expansion of the space between the molecules, the molecules move upwards and the upper layer molecules comes downward due to the movement of the heated molecules upwards, and then these recently send molecules, with the heated surface gets heat and again goes up, replacing another layer of molecules. Thus like this the convection currents flows and heat transfer occurs in a free convection. It is also called as Natural convection.

2.ii Forced convection

The type of convection in which we put external forces on the fluids for the convection currents to flow and cause convection. And, since the fluid is forced to do convection, this type of convection is called forced convection. Take the example of a fireplace where near it, you are sitting and you are given the task of pumping air into fire. Why do we do it? We do it so that the air just pumped reaches the fire and through radiation it gets heated which cause them to spread throughout the room, making the room warmer. This also one application of the Forced convection.

The Property of the anomalous expansion of water and convection is also responsible for saving the lives of the aquatic animals at the colder countries. For more information you can refer to the chapter of Thermal expansion, in the topic of *Anomalous expansion of water*.

3. Radiation

Why do we get heat from a fire place? Why do we feel hot in a kitchen? Its because of the radiation of heat. Radiation is the transfer of heat without any medium. So this implies that in vacuum also heat can be transferred through radiation, just like sun does. Radiations are electromagnetic waves.

3.1 Prevost's theory of Exchange

It is one of the most important theory of Radiation which tells us that :

- All body emits heat radiation at all temperatures. Thus, amount of radiation emitted depends on the temperature and material. So, if the temperature of the body is more in comparison to the surrounding, the body will emit more heat radiation.
- All body absorbs heat radiation at every temperatures. Thus, amount of radiation absorbed also depends on the temperature and material. So, if the temperature of the surroundings is more the body will absorb more

Thus rate of radiation emitted by a body is equivalent to the rate of radiation absorbed.

3.2 Emissive Power (E)

Suppose that you have a body which is emitting radiations . Let the body be 'A'. Let it emit Q energy from an area A in time t . It emits this energy in a solid angle ω . Thus we can say that:

$Q \propto A$

$Q \propto \omega$

Q∝ t

∴ Q = EAωt, where E is the emissive power of the body and also the proportionality constant. Thus in the differential form it can also be expressed for a small amount of energy coming from a very small solid angle, from a very small area and in a very small time, we get,

dQ=E dA dω dt

or,

dQ/dA dt = E dω

or,

Power/Area =E dω

or,

Intensity of heat radiations emitted = E dω

Suppose a body is heated first at a moderate temperature and then at a higher temperature, it will certainly radiate heat but at different rates and of different wavelengths at different temperature , you can see that the body obtains different colors, if seen from a heat detecting machine, the body's color's wavelength will decrease with respect to temperature increase, which implies that as the temperature of a body increases the heat is emitted more of a particular wavelength shorter than the previous temperature. This is **Spectral emissive power** which is described as the emissive power of the wavelength of light which is radiated at maximum by the body emitting the radiations. This is also the root of Wien's displacement law 3.7.

3.3 Absorptive Power (a)

Take the example of body that is absorbing heat radiations. For the sake of consideration, we can assumme that 100 radiations are falling on it , out of which it absorbs 500 radiations out of the 1000 radiations, and the rest of the 500 radiations are reflected back by the body. So as it absorbs 500 out of 1000 radiation, it absorptive power is given by:

absorptive power (a)= no. of radiations absorbed/ no. of radiations incidented

So, here the absorptive power of the object we are talking about is 0.5.

Sometimes, the body emits some radiations of some specific wavelengths of light which means that at different temperature it will absorb different wavelength of light radiations. As the temperature becomes lower of the body absorbing radiations, more the body will absorb radiations, and that too of the lower wavelengths of light. So, **Spectral**

Absorptive power is the absorption of the particular radiation of the particular wavelength of light by the body.

Note: When one body is cooled more, then it absorbs more heat than radiating (emitting) heat and when the same is heated more then it radiates (emits) more amount of heat than absorbing.

3.4 Black Body

The term black body was introduced by Gustav Kirchhoff in 1860. It is an ideal concept. In practical situations, we cannot create a perfect black body. So, Black body is that kind of body that absorbs all radiation falling on it at any temperature and at any incident angle. Thus we can infer from this, that the black body does not either transmit the heat radiations or reflect the heat radiations incidented to it. Thus the absorptive power of a ideal black body is always 1. These types of highly absorptive bodies are named as black bodies since black color is good absorber, but this does not mean that every black body should be black. <u>Everybody that absorbs every radiations falling on it at all temperature and at any incident angle is a black body.</u> The black bodies also emits maximum heat radiations. Just like a star, or a isothermal enclosure[see Fig. 5], black painted platinum etc.

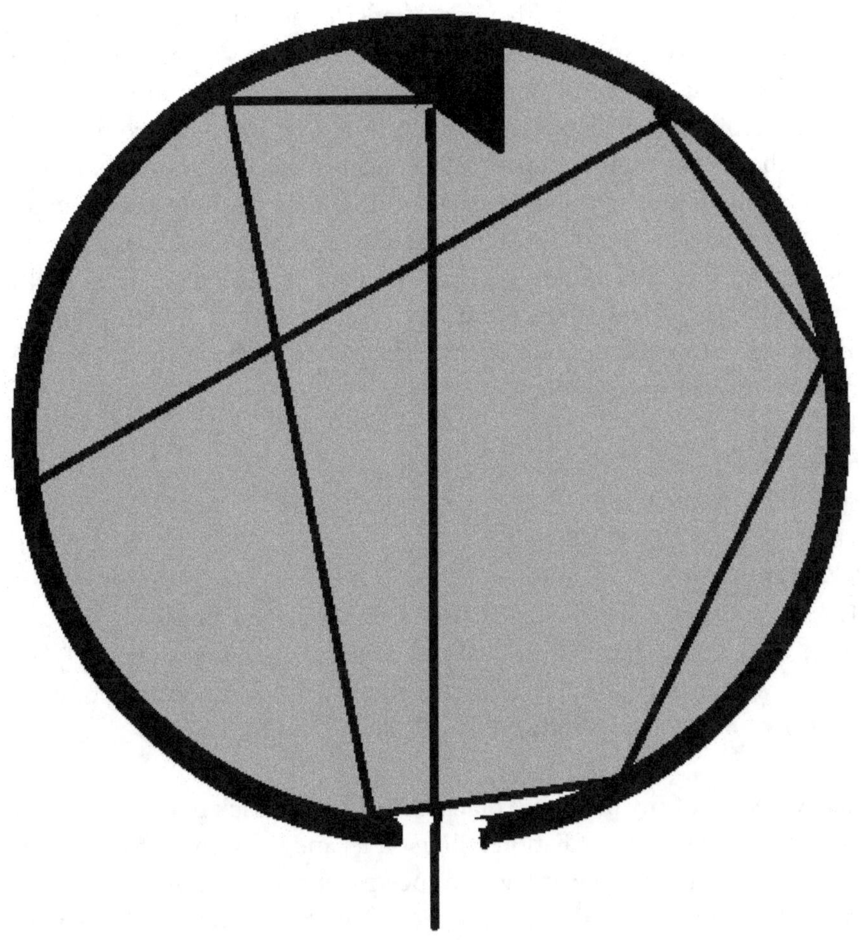

Fig.5 an isothermal enclosure

As you can see that the radiation is first incidented through a source, the radiation goes in the body through a very minute opening, and then it is trapped in the enclosure because of an aperture , preventing the radiation to reflect back and go through the very small opening.

3.5 Kirchoff's law

When a body can absorb heat radiations very easily then the body can even emit radiations also very easily. Consider that you are studying a topic very seriously and with your utmost concentration. By studying more and more, you gain more and more confidence in yourself. Here, you are absorbing more and more knowledge. Now if you are asked tell about that topic in your respective institution. You feel very comfortable to speak about that topic because your concepts are very clear about that topic. You will emit every knowledge about that topic that you have studied about that topic. This is not directly related to Kirchoff's law, but it can be however helpful to understand it. Thus the Law of Kirchoff , states that a good absorber is a good emitter and vice - versa. Thus if E high then a is high, and if E is low then a is low. This is also same fo the spectral versions of the former quantities.

Thus,

$E \propto a$

Spectral $E \propto$ Spectral a

Thus,

$E / a = $ constant

This is applicable for every body, and even for a black body.

Now, as we know that an ideal black body has $a = 1$, so as we know E/a is a constant we can state that E/a of any is equal to E/a of the black body

$\therefore$ **E(any body)/a(any body)=E(black body)/a(black body)**

or,

E(any body)/a(any body)=E(black body) [$\because$ a (black body)=1 because blackbody absorbs every radiation falling on it] and the same is for the ratio of the spectral emissive power and the spectral absorptive power.

$\therefore$**spectral E(any body)/spectral a(any body)=spectral E(black body)/spectral a(black body)**

or,

spectral E(any body)/spectral a(any body)=spectral E(black body) [$\because$ spectral a (black body)=1]

Note: The temperature of the surroundings is same as it is around the black body and the heat radiation provided is also same.

3.6 Black body Radiations

Consider two identical bodies, where both are black bodies. Now, they are kept in two different rooms where they are set at different temperatures. The temperature of the surroundings should be the same in both of the rooms. You will see that the black body in a higher temperature radiates heats the room at a faster rate than the black body at the lower temperature and as we know the higher the amount of heat lower is the wavelength i.e. λ of which we receive the maximum amount. So from this, we can also infer that higher the temperature of the black body, lower is the wavelength of the maximum amount of that radiation, because heat is directly proportional to the temperature of a body, more precisely the temperature difference of the body. This is called as:

3.6.1 Wien's displacement Law

As we have seen in the topic of black body radiations (3.6) we now know that,

$\lambda \propto 1/T$, where λ is the wavelength of radiation and T is the temperature of the body.

Now, let's consider a constant b, which is also called as **Wien's constant**.

So, as

$\lambda \propto 1/T$,

$\lambda = b/T$

or,

$\lambda T = b$

where b's value is $2.8977 *10^{-3}$ m-K [metre(m)*Kelvin(K)], its also the proportionality constant as well as an universal constant.

Now,

For the other black bodies we can tell that,

$\lambda T = \lambda` T` = \lambda`` T`` = b$.................[where $\lambda`$, $\lambda``$ are the wavelengths coming out in the form of radiation in maximum amount and $T`$, $T``$ are the temperatures of other black bodies]

Other bodies (except ideal black bodies) also follow wien's law but not very ideally.

Now lets understand why is it called as Wien's **Displacement** law with the help of a simple graph:

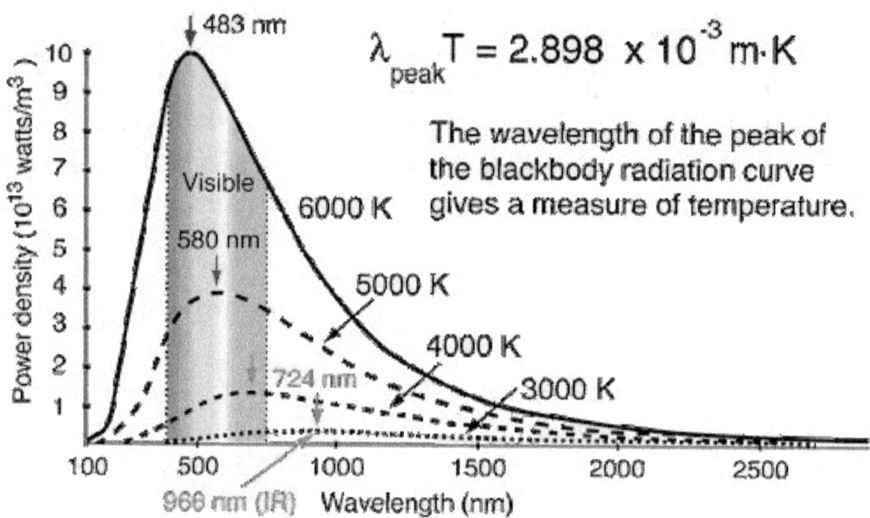

As we can see in the graph that as the temperature increases the intensity of the radiations having lower wavelength increase. Thus we can say that the value of λmax is **Displaced** towards the lower wavelengths as the temperature is increased of that black body or any other body.

3.7 Stefan-Boltzmann Law

It was formulated in 1879 by Austrian physicist Josef Stefan as a result of his experimental studies, the same law was derived in 1884 by Austrian physicist Ludwig Boltzmann from thermodynamic considerations. Josef Stefan observed that when a perfectly black body emits radiation, it will emit all the radiation it has in it, because its a black body, and when we heat this black body more and more, the black body's radiation energy also increase, and by experiments he discovered that the intensity of the radiations emitted by the black body is directly proportional to the fourth power of Temperature of that same black body. So we express it as:

$Q/At \propto T^4$

let the proportionality constant be σ.

so,

$Q/t = \sigma AT^4$

=>Power radiated = σAT^4................for a perfectly black body

From Kirchoff's law,

we can say that,

for any other body's emissive power we can express it as:

E(any body)/E(ideal black body)=a (the same random body)............where the E term is the power radiated in this case. Since we are considering a normal body, we have to consider a rate of energy that would be emitted by the normal body, because it can't emit every energy radiation in it, like a black body. So let that rate be ε.

=>$(\varepsilon*\sigma AT^4)/\sigma AT^4 = a$

=>$\varepsilon = a$

Now from the above expression we can clearly understand this rate is equal to the absorptive power of a body, so, since black body has its absorptive power as 1, the power radiated by it is always σAT^4,

So the perfect expression for Stefan's law is,

Power radiated = $\varepsilon\sigma AT^4$, where $0\leq\varepsilon\leq1$, ε is named as emissivity.

And if there is a surrounding's temperature that is affecting the power radiated, then we write it as:

Net Power Radiated = $\varepsilon\sigma AT^4 - \varepsilon\sigma A(Ts)^4$ (where Ts is the surrounding temperature)........it actually expresses that the energy radiated by the black body or any other body subtracted from the energy already present in the surroundings.

and after taking the common factors in this equation, we get,

Net Power Radiated = $\varepsilon\sigma A\{T^4 - (Ts)^4\}$

in Stefan's law , σ is also referred to as the Stefan's constant, whose value is $5.67 * 10^{-8}$ Watt(W)/metre^2(m^2) Kelvin^4 (K^4) or, $\sigma= 5.67 * 10^{-8}$ W/m^2 K^4.

3.8 Newton's law of cooling

Isaac Newton published his work on cooling anonymously in 1701 as 'Scala graduum Caloris'. Rather, using today's terms, Newton noted after some mathematical manipulation, the rate of temperature change of a body is proportional to the difference in temperatures between the body and its surroundings and this implies that with time the temperature difference between the body and the surroundings decreases leading to an equilibrium. Thus,

Rate of cooling $\propto \Delta Tbs$, where ΔTbs means the temperature of the body- the temperature of the surroundings,

we can also write it in the form of,

$\Delta T/\Delta t \propto \Delta Tbs$

or, in differential form,

dT/dt ∝ ΔTbs,

or,

dT/dt ∝ Tb-Ts, where Tb is the temperature of the body and Ts is the temperature of the surroundings.

<u>Proof(dT/dt ∝ Tb-Ts)</u> :

From Stefan's law,

we have the eqn.:

dQ/dt = εσA{(Tb)^4 - (Ts)^4}

=>mcdT/dt = εσA{(Tb)^4 - (Ts)^4} [here, replaced dQ by mcdT, from the formula of dQ=mcdT, see chapter 8 Calorimetry]

=>dT/dt ={εσA/mc}{Tb^4 - (Ts)^4} [let εσA/mc =K]

=>dT/dt =K{Tb^4 - (Ts)^4} [since ΔTbs=Tb-Ts]

=>dT/dt =K{(ΔTbs+Ts)^4 - (Ts)^4}

=>dT/dt =K{((ΔTbs/Ts+1)(Ts))^4 - (Ts)^4}

=>dT/dt =K(Ts)^4 ((ΔTbs/Ts+1)^4 - 1)..............[using (1+x)^n=1+nx, because here if we consider(ΔTbs/Ts+1), then ΔTbs/Ts is much smaller than 1]

So, this now becomes,

=>dT / dt =K (Ts)^4 ((1 + 4(ΔTbs / Ts) - 1)

=>dT / dt =K (Ts)^4 (4 ΔTbs / Ts)

=>dT/dt = 4K(Ts)^3(Tb - Ts)

Thus by this, we get that the rate of cooling is directly proportional to the temperature difference between the the body and the surroundings. Be careful with this, that the temperatures should be at kelvin otherwise if given in any other units , convert it into kelvin.

Now, consider a body kept in a place. It is radiating heat in the room, so its temperature will decrease. See Fig. 6 :

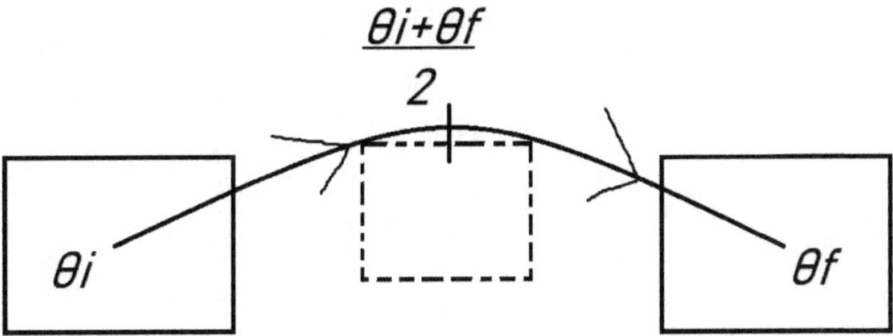

Fig.6 showing the temperature change with respect to the surroundings.

Considering that in Δt time is in the surroundings of θs temperature ,
we assume the temperature of the body (Tb) as $(\theta i+\theta f)/2$, as the temperature of the body, when it is halfway to reach the thermal equilibrium,
So we now get from Newton's law of Cooling , that,
$\Delta T/\Delta t \propto \Delta Tbs$
$\Delta T/\Delta t \propto Tb\text{-}Ts$
$\theta f\text{-}\theta i/\Delta t \propto ((\theta i+\theta f)/2)\text{-}\theta s$
$=>\theta f\text{-}\theta i/\Delta t = L\ [((\theta i+\theta f)/2)\text{-}\theta s\ ]$.......................[where L is a constant of Proportionality]
This equation can be used for general purposes, and Remember that it is an consideration made here above. The formula usefull in all situations and conditions is the below:
$dT/dt = 4(\varepsilon\sigma A/mc)(Ts)^3(Tb - Ts)$ [Consider $L = 4(\varepsilon\sigma A/mc)(Ts)^3$,it's the constant]

Part-3 The Waves

Chapters:-

10) Basics of Oscillations [more about this in the upcoming books]

11) Mechanical Waves

12) How did we measure the speed of Light?

13) Some Wave and Particle phenomena

We will continue for the part of electromagnetic waves in the book Ask-Physics 4, till then we can enjoy the mechanical waves part....

CHAPTER TEN

Basics of Oscillations

What are Oscilations?

Have you seen a boy/girl jumping on a trampoline? I guess yes, We have seen it right.....Or, even sometimes in the olden clocks we see a pendulum like structure at the transparent bottom. They move in **to** and **fro** type of motion. In this type of motion, we can see an object going forwards and then backwards after specific periods of time which are equal, or more simply we can tell that the body(object) is repeating its motion after equal intervals of time. This is called as **Oscillation** or **the Oscillatory motion.** This type of motion falls in the category of Periodic motion. We should remember that every oscillation is a periodic motion but every periodic motion is not an oscillation because in oscillation we have an equilibrium position whereas in periodic motions it is not necessary to have an equilibriumposition. Some examples of oscillation includes the revolution of earth around the sun, the to and fro movement of the Pendulum, etc. And, in Periodic motion we have examples of the string of guitar or violin or even of sitar when it is plucked etc. They even include examples of oscillation.

Now in oscillation we calculate the restoring force acting on the body throughout the motion, through the formula:

$F = -kx^n$, where n is any integer, k is a constant, namely the spring constant and x is the displacement of the particle in oscillatory motion from the mean position and F is the force applied to bring the particle back to the mean positions. When the power of x, or more precisely 'n' is 1 then we say it as the **Simple Harmonic motion,** and the formula becomes $F = -kx$. With this we have many terms associated. They include angular frequency, phase difference, Amplitude etc.

We even have two types of oscillations, they are:

1) **Damped Oscillations**

The oscillations which gets diminished due to the non conservative forces' influence is called as Damped oscillations. For example we have a pendulum and have placed it inside the water tumbler containing water and have suspended it outside such that the bob and some part of the string is immersed in water. Now when we disturb the pendulum the simple harmonic motion doesn't last for long. This shows that due to the fluid friction which is a non conservative force that acts on the pendulum, the pendulum is brought stable to its mean position in a very short period of time.

2) Undamped Oscillations

The oscillations which doesn't get diminished is called as Undamped oscillations. For example we have a pendulum and this time it is in vacuum. Now when we disturb the bob of the pendulum the motion of the pendulum will go on. It will never stop and will never ever come to its mean position.

Note that every Oscillatory motion is not a SHM(Simple Harmonic Motion). But every SHM is a Oscillatory motion. Rather It (SHM) is a special case of Oscillatory motion.

3) Forced Oscillations

Consider a particular situation where you have a string strecthed and hanged straight and two identical bob and string system connected at a distance from each other. Considering all the other to be ideal, we disturb one pendulum out of the two. What do we observe? That's pretty intuitive. The second pendulum is forced to oscillate by the force applied by the disturbed pendulum which is in fact external to it. The natural frequency[to be read in chapter 12] of two pendulums are same as they are identical. The driving force has the driving frequency same as that of the natural frequency of these pendulums. This is called **Resonance**. This is special case of forced oscillations. Now if in the same case the properties of the pendulums like their shapes and sizes were changed, then the driving force of the disturbed pendulum is uncapable of driving the pendulum at rest, at its natural frequency, and thus the amplitude is less. Therefore, **Forced oscillations** are those oscillations where an external driving force acts on a body from another oscillating body, makes it move in an oscillatory motion.

Some common defintions in SHM and their derivations

The extreme position on both the sides of the mean position uptill which the particle can oscillate are called as the **Amplitudes** of the particle. The time required by the particle to cover one cycle of oscillation is called as the Time period of the particle in SHM. The **Angular frequency** of the particle is the Scalar quantity that tells us that how quick it had covered the cycle of 2π radians or in other words it is the measure of the oscillation rate of a particle and that's why we multiply the linear frequency 'v' to 2π radians which means 360 degrees or the total angle of a circle. The more quick it will cover the the cycle of 2π radians the more will be its frequency and angular frequency. Thus, this leads us to the conclusion of an equation that the Angular frequency 'ω' is indirectly proportional to time 'T', therefore $\omega = 2\pi/ T$, or we can even write it as $\omega = 2\pi v$, because $v = 1/ T$. There is a frequency v because it has a time period, just as in Waves, where the particles travel in some specific time and when this is multiplied to the wavelength of the wave [see Chapter 11] we get the velocity of the Wave. So similarly here also we multiply the the 2π radians with the frequency to get the 'angular' frequency so that we can get the frequency of the particle doing SHM in a angular mode. We also get the expression of a=-(ω^2)x from F=-kx, by comparing F=ma and then by considering ω=$\sqrt{(k/m)}$, or ω^2=k/m .[Proof will be given later for this, in this chapter]

Now let us consider that the particle is at the mean position where x=0 and t=0. So, at t=t(and t≠0) we get that the particle is at a point x, away from the mean position, we have the amplitude of it as A. Now from the eqn. a=-(ω^2)x, on writing the differential form of it (acceleration) a=v(dv/dx), we equate it with -(ω^2)x, and then we get it as:

v(dv/dx)=(ω^2)x [we are only considering the magnitude not the direction of quantities]

=>v dv = (ω^2)x dx

Integrating both the sides in LHS we integrate from 0 to v and in RHS we integrate from x to A,

we get,

=>(v^2)/2= (ω^2)(A^2 - x^2)/2

=>v^2=(ω^2)(A^2 - x^2)

=>v=$\sqrt{(($\omega$^2)(A^2 - x^2))}$

=>v=±ω $\sqrt{(A^2 - x^2)}$

the above two highlighted equations can be used for calculating the velocity of the particle in SHM.

Now, if we again write v=dx/dt

=>dx/dt = ±ω $\sqrt{(A^2 - x^2)}$

=>∫ dx/$\sqrt{(A^2 - x^2)}$ = ±ω ∫ dt.............[integrating from 0 to x in the LHS and integrating from 0 to t in RHS]

$$=> \arcsin(x/A) \quad - \quad 0 \quad = \quad \pm\omega t \quad -$$
$$0 \dotfill [\arcsin \text{ of } x/A \text{ means sin inverse of } x/A]$$

$=> x/A = \sin(\pm\omega t)$

$=> \mathbf{x = A\ sin(\pm\omega t)}$ ....(i)

Now, from the equation of $\int dx/\sqrt{(A^2 - x^2)} = \pm\omega \int dt$, if we take the limits in the LHS as from A to x meaning the particle is starting its oscillations from its amplitude and take limits in the RHS from 0 to t , during integration ,then it becomes the following:

$=> \arcsin(x/A) - \arcsin(A/A) = \pm\omega t - 0$

$=> \arcsin(x/A) - \arcsin(1) = \pm\omega t$

$=> \arcsin(x/A) - 90 = \pm\omega t$ $[\because \arcsin(1) = 90]$

$=> \arcsin(x/A) = 90 \pm\omega t$

$=> x/A = \sin(90 \pm\omega t)$

$=> x = A \sin(90 \pm\omega t)$ $[\because \sin(90 \pm\omega t) = \cos(\pm\omega t)]$

$=> \mathbf{x = A\ cos(\pm\omega t)}$ ....(ii)

So, the equations (i) and (ii) are the equations of SHM, from which we can calculate the value of x of the particle from the mean position. Sometimes what happens is that the particle is already at a certain point else away from mean position and for that we add the initial phase of the particle Φ to $\pm\omega t$ and here by initial phase we mean that the particle's position before the SHM starts, resulting into the formulae $x = A \sin(\pm\omega t \pm\Phi)$, and $x = A \cos(\pm\omega t \pm\Phi)$. Now since we know that when we differentiate x with respect to time we get velocity the same is here, what we do is that, we differentiate x of the particle from the mean position of the particle with respect time. We get:

$\partial x/\partial t = \partial(A \sin(\pm\omega t \pm\Phi))/\partial t$

$=> \mathbf{v = A\ \omega\ cos\ (\pm\omega t \pm\Phi)}$

Or, if we first consider the $x = A \cos(\pm\omega t \pm\Phi)$

Then we will get it to be,

$=> \mathbf{v = -\ A\ \omega\ sin(\pm\omega t \pm\Phi)}$

Or,

Again, differentiating this quantity with respect time, we get the acceleration of the particle:

$\partial v/\partial t = \partial(A \omega \cos (\pm\omega t \pm\Phi))/\partial t$

$=> \mathbf{a = -A\ (\omega^2)\ sin(\pm\omega t \pm\Phi)}$

And, for $v = -A \omega \sin(\pm\omega t \pm\Phi)$, we get the acceleration to be:

$\partial v/\partial t = \partial(- A \omega \sin(\pm\omega t\pm\Phi))/\partial t$

$=>a = - A (\omega^2) \cos(\pm\omega t\pm\Phi)$

Or,

a= $(-\omega^2)x$, because the value of x is A $\sin(\pm\omega t\pm\Phi)$ or A $\cos(\pm\omega t\pm\Phi)$

The term of $\pm\omega t\pm\Phi$ is called as the phase of the particle, where Φ is the initial phase.

The Differential form of the SHM equation:

Since we know that the equation a=$(-\omega^2)x$ depicts the acceleration of the paricle in SHM.

We also know that a=d(dx/dt)/dt

$\therefore$ As,

a=a

$=>d(dx/dt)/dt=(-\omega^2)x$

$=>(dx/dt)/dt + (\omega^2)x = 0$ ....differential form of SHM equation of acceleration.

Now as accordance to the equation of ' a = -A (ω^2) $\sin(\pm\omega t\pm\Phi)$ ', we can see here that the previous equation for x we derived, is the same present in the equation for the acceleration in SHM of the particle. So we can write it as a = $(-\omega^2)x$ and now we also know that F=-kx =ma , so , we can say that a from this can be said as -kx/m, so on equating a= $(-\omega^2)x$ with a= -kx/m we get:

$(-\omega^2)x = -kx/m$

$=>(\omega^2)x = kx/m$

$=> (\omega^2) = k/m$

or,

$=>\omega = \sqrt{(k/m)}$

Here, in all of these equations the value of Φ can't be smaller than 0 and cannot be greater than 2π.

$\therefore 0 \leq \Phi \leq 2\pi$

Proof of T=2π/ω

We get an equation of |x|=|x*|,where x is the displacement of the particle towards the +A and x* is the same displacement, in magnitude, of the particle in the -A, as the distances from the mean position is the same and even their velocities and accelerations are also same because they are at the same <u>elevations</u> from the ground <u>**(if considered a simple pendulum working under the force of gravity)**</u>. This also valid for the cases where the driving force or the restoring is other than gravity. So as we have derived and understood that why x is equal to A $\sin(\omega t+\Phi)$, so putting the values of x* and x, where the particle takes t+T time to reach the position of x*,

we get,

$|x|=|x*|$

$=>|A \sin(\omega t+\Phi)| = |-A \sin(\omega(t+T)+\Phi)|$

$=>\sin(\omega t+\Phi)=\sin(\omega(t+T)+\Phi)$

Now, let $\alpha = \omega t + \Phi$ and let $\theta = \omega(t+T) + \Phi$

$\therefore \sin\alpha=\sin\theta$

So the probabilities for having $\sin\alpha=\sin\theta$ are 3, that are:

i) $\theta = \alpha$

ii) **$\theta = 2\pi + \alpha$**

iii) $\theta = \pi - \alpha$

Now since the points are same in magnitude then the velocities also must be same in magnitude,

$|v| = |v*|$ where v is the velocity of the particle in SHM towards the +A and v* is the velocity of the particle in SHM towards -A. So as we have derived and understood that why v is equal to A $\omega \cos(\omega t+\Phi)$ so putting the values of v* and v, where the particle takes t+T time to reach the position of v*,

so we get,

$|v| = |v*|$

$=>|A \omega \cos(\omega t+\Phi)| = |-A \omega \cos(\omega(t+T)+\Phi)|$

$=>\cos(\omega t+\Phi) = \cos(\omega(t+T)+\Phi)$

Now again, let $\alpha = \omega t + \Phi$ and let $\theta = \omega(t+T) + \Phi$

Now we get it as,

$=> \cos\alpha=\cos\theta$

So the probabilities for having $\cos\alpha=\cos\theta$ are again 3, that are:

i) $\theta = \alpha$

ii) **$\theta = 2\pi + \alpha$**

iii) $\theta = 2\pi - \alpha$

So we can now see that except $\theta = \alpha$, we also one more common factor that is $\theta = 2\pi + \alpha$, so we can say that

$\theta = \theta$

$=> 2\pi + \alpha = \omega(t+T)+\Phi$

$=> 2\pi + \omega t + \Phi = \omega t + \omega T + \Phi$

$=> 2\pi = \omega T$

$=> \omega = 2\pi/T$ ....**for angular frequency** or,

=> **T = 2π/ω**..................................**for Time period of a particle or body in SHM**

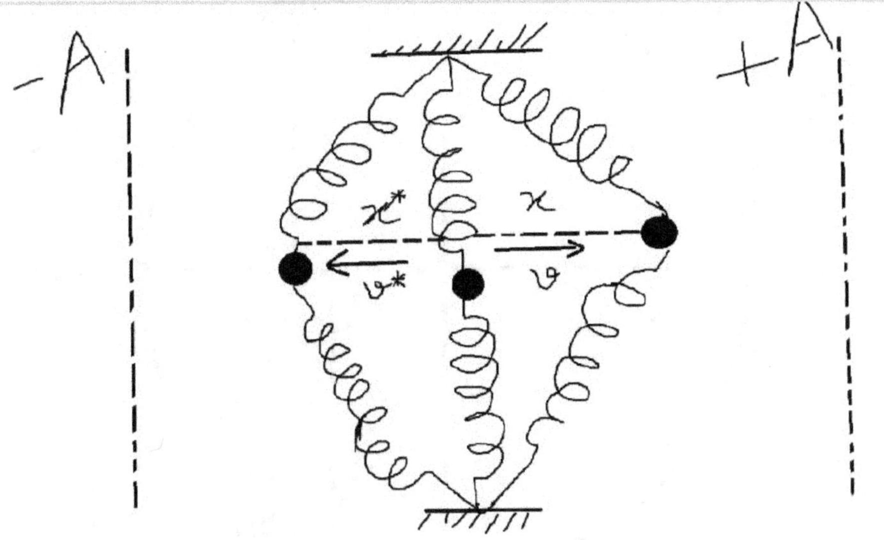

Fig.1 showing the experiment used to deduce the Value of T=2π/ω

<u>Phasor Diagrams</u>

Imagine a particle doing SHM in a circular path, we see that when it does SHM in that circular path, which actually means that this particle is moving in that circular path, it first starts from O then goes to a, then to b, then to d and then to c.

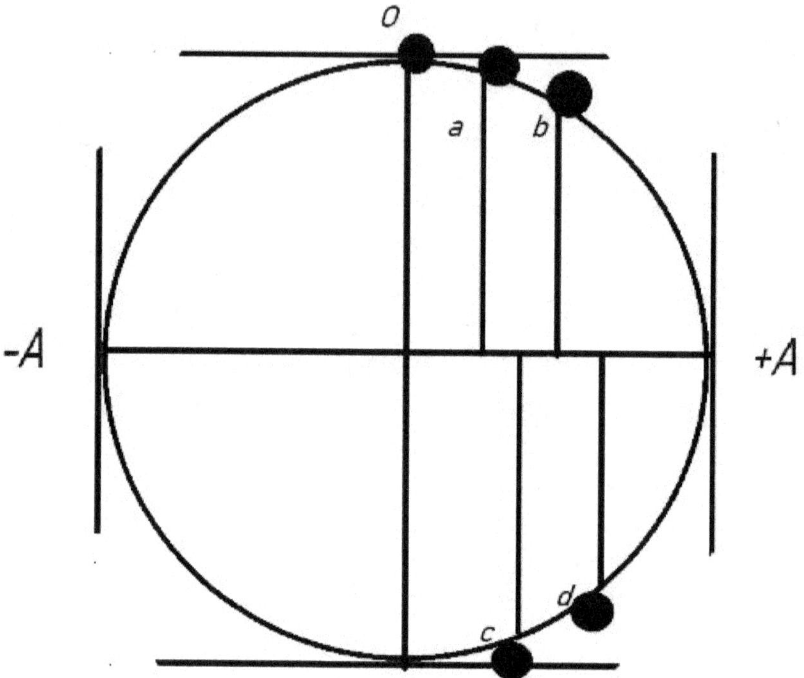

Fig. 2 - can be used for guiding one's imagination.

So we see here that the particle going from a to c in a circular representation. The thing to observe is that the particle moves from a and then after sometime it reaches a position just opposite a which is same in magnitude also, and it's not c. Thus it is moving to and fro about its mean position O. But, this does not mean that the particle is doing SHM. We have to prove it. So, let's do it.....

Now consider that in that circular representation the particle just moves to a, so if we join that point a with the centre of the circle then the radius of the circle is found and because the radius of the circle is the the amplitude of the periodic motion of that same particle we name this new line as A and as A makes an angle or angular displacement 'θ' with the point from where the particle started doing its motion; we can say that the measure of the displacement as $A \sin\theta$, after breaking the components of A. Now for theta we can say that it is also the angular displacement covered by the particle. So from Chapter 3, we learnt that Angular displacement 'θ' is equal to the

Angular frequency 'ω' times the Time taken by the particle 't' to cover that angular displacement . Therefore the equation of the displacement of the particle becomes A sinωt, and because x=A sinωt is one of the equations of the SHM, therefore now it's proved that the particle is doing SHM. "Why do we Use or Need Phasor Diagrams?" would be one of the probable questions in your mind, and thus is needed to be answered. We use it because it makes the imagination and visualization of SHM easier and for the initial phase of SHM we just need here a thought that the particle having an initial phase would be at a position where x≠0 according to the convention. So by this we can even calculate the initial phase of the particle. See Fig 3 :

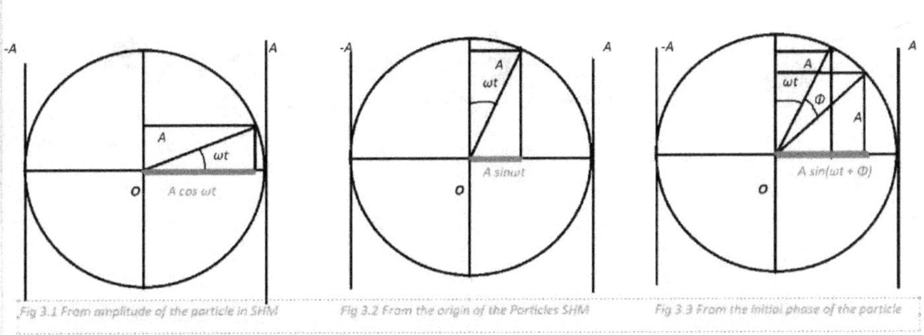

Fig.3 Shows the Possible types of Phasor Diagram

Energy in SHM

Consider a particle doing SHM about a Mean Position O and and reaching the Amplitude A and Amplitude -A. Now when we are talking about energy in the Particle it is always conserved it in every particle until and unless any non-conservative forces such as frictional force, tension, magnetic force etc. , act on it.

Now we are going to talk about the Mechanical energy of the particle due to which the different quanties like the acceleration, the velocity and as well the total energy present in the particle differs.

- **Potential energy of the Particle in SHM**

The potential energy of the particle changes at every point. It is the energy which is gained or possessed by the particle or the body . Normally we say that the potential energy can be defined by the formula of U=mgh, but this is not true. We can only define the change in the potential energy in the body or the particle by the formula of ΔU = -Wc, where 'ΔU' is the change in potential energy of the body and 'Wc' in the work done by the conservative force(s). We can understand the concept of potential energy with the help of a sponge, where when we squeeze it the air comes out or we can say that it is expended and when we leave it the air come in again , or it gains the air, here the sponge is the body, and air is the potential energy. This is a type of demonstration that can be used to understand how the particle gains P.E. and how it loses it. See Fig. 4

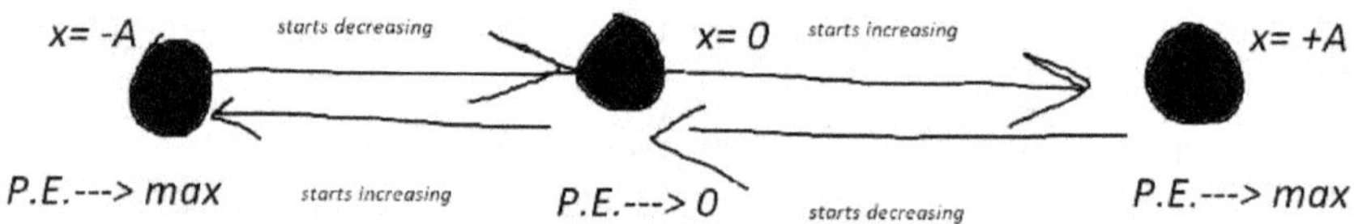

Fig. 4 Showing the variations in the P.E. of a particle in SHM

Now let's derive the formula for P.E.

Since here in this system the spring force is a conservative force, we can write as mentioned earlier about it, i.e.:

ΔU = -Wc

or,

dU = -F dx cosθ

Since here the force of spring acts in the opposite direction it makes an angle of π radians or 180 degrees.

∴ dU = -F dx cos(π)

=> dU = F dx [because cos(π)= - 1 and -1*(-1)=1]

=> dU = k (x dx)

Now integrating (U^0) with respect to dU from U to U* where U is the potential energy at the mean position and U * is the potential energy at any point x and we also integrate the quantity (x^1) with respect to dx from 0 to x.

we obtain,

=> U* - U = k[(x^2)/2]

=> U* = U + k (x^2)/2

In most of the cases we consider the Potential Energy at the mean position to be zero , but this case is not always the same sometimes if the system is not isolated then the Potential energy of the particle is a non zero value. It is a scalar quantity.

As the formula suggests the P.E. is maximum at the Amplitudes, where it becomes, ±(0.5)(k)(A^2) and is minimum at the mean position where it becomes zero.

- **Kinetic Energy of the Particle in SHM**

When the particle moves with a higher velocity we say that the particle has higher potential energy and when the particle is moving with a lower velocity we say that the particle has less kinetic energy. Similarly in the SHM of a particle the quantities like velocity , acceleration and displacement oscillate, as their value oscillates like a wave. That's a different part. The thing that is wanted to be conveyed is that the value of kinetic energy of a particle in SHM varies (and doesn't oscillate as well as P.E. even varies but doesn't oscillate) . It varies like in Fig. 5. At the mean position it is maximum and at the amplitudes the value of the K.E. (Kinetic Energy) is zero. Observe the Fig. 5 below.

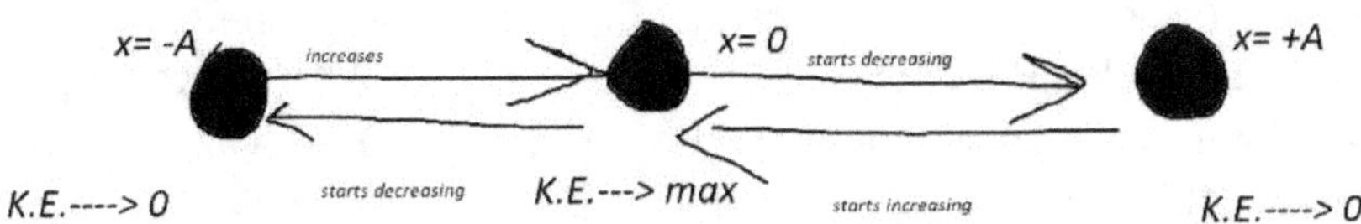

Fig. 5 Showing the variations in the K.E. of a particle in SHM

Now, let's derive the formula for the Kinetic energy of a particle in SHM. So, first we apply the formula of K.E. = (0.5)(m v^2)

According to this formula,

=> K.E. = (0.5)(m(ω^2)(A^2 - x^2)).................... [using v^2 = (ω^2)(A^2 - x^2)]

=>K.E. = (0.5)(m(ω^2)(A^2 - x^2))...............[using the formula ω^2 = k/m]

=>K.E. = (0.5)(m(k/m)(A^2 - x^2))

=>K.E. = (0.5)(k)(A^2 - x^2)

we can even state the K.E. as,

K.E. = (0.5)(m v^2)

=> K.E. = (0.5)(m)(A^2)(ω^2)[cos(ωt±Φ)]^2............[using v = A ω cos(ωt±Φ)]

or,

=> K.E. = (0.5)(k)(A^2)[cos(ωt±Φ)]^2...............[using ω^2 = k/m]

The above two highlighted equations may be used for finding the kinetic energy of the particle.

- **Total mechanical energy in SHM**

When the particle does the SHM, it gains and loses Potential and Kinetic Energy simultaneously . So if on one hand the Potential energy increases then obviously the Kinetic energy decreases, and if the Potential energy decreases then the Kinetic energy will increase for sure. And we also know that as the particle here is only acted upon by a conservative force, therefore the total mechanical energy is always conserved here in the particle during its SHM. Therefore the total mechanical energy can be written as:

Total mechanical energy = Potential Energy + Kinetic Energy

=> Total mechanical energy =(U + k (x^2)/2) + ((0.5)(k)(A^2 - x^2))

=> Total mechanical energy =(U + k (x^2)/2) + ((0.5)(k)(A^2) - (0.5)(k)(x^2))

=> Total mechanical energy = U + (0.5)(k)(A^2)

And when we consider the initial P.E. of the particle as zero the term U becomes 0, So the Total Mechanical Energy of the Particle in SHM is:

Total mechanical energy = (0.5)(k)(A^2)

Now observe the graph of the variations of Kinetic Energy and Potential Energy Carefully, In this the Graph 1 shows the graph for the particle having a non-zero initial Potential energy, Graph 2 shows the graph for the particle having a zero initial Potential energy and the Graph 3 shows the graph of the variations in the Kinetic energy of the particle in SHM.

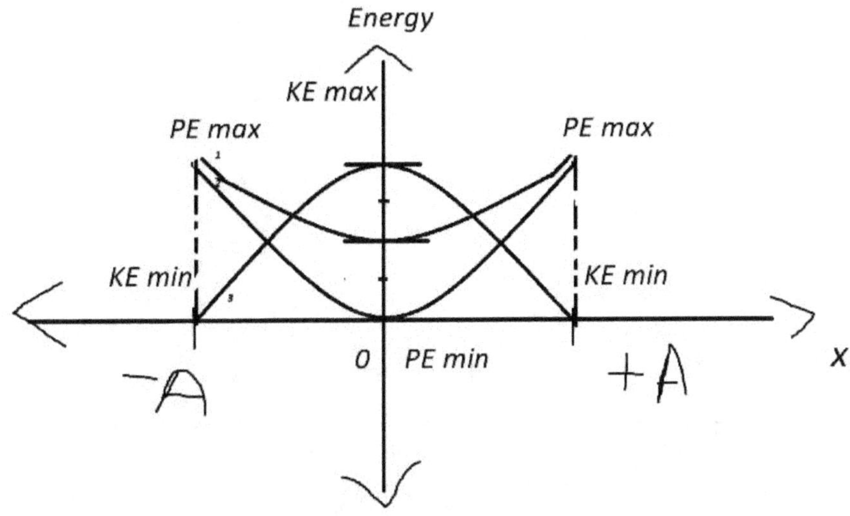

The Graphs in SHM

1. For F v/s x

When the particle does the SHM the particle is pulled by a conservative force in the opposite direction to the displacement of the particle. Therefore when the particle is moving in the -ve x direction, it will have a force positive and the particle moving in +ve direction of x, will have a force trying to bring it to the mean position.

Since the formula of F in a SHM is F= -kx, therefore the graph of it is like this:

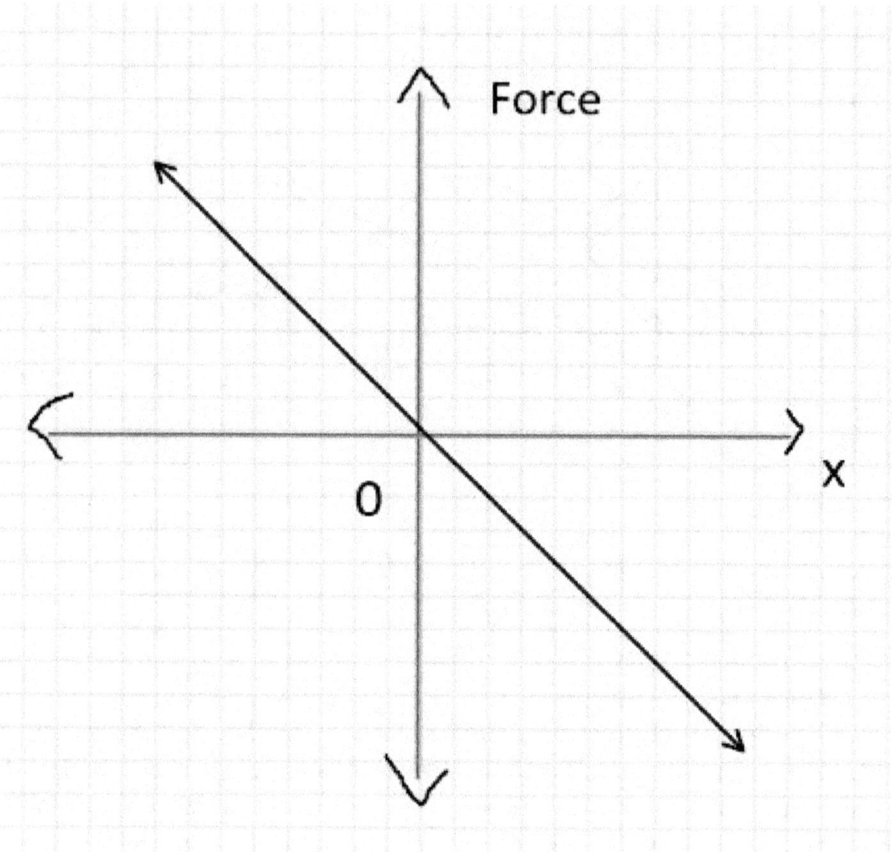

2. For a v/s x

When the particle does the SHM the particle is pulled by a conservative force in the opposite direction to the displacement of the particle. Therefore when the particle is moving in the -ve x direction, it will have a force positive which means an acceleration positive,due to the force acting on the particle, and the particle when moving in +ve direction of x, it will have a force negative, which means an acceleration negative,due to the force acting on the particle, trying to bring it to the mean position.

Since the formula of a in a SHM is a= -(ω^2)x, therefore the graph of it is like this:

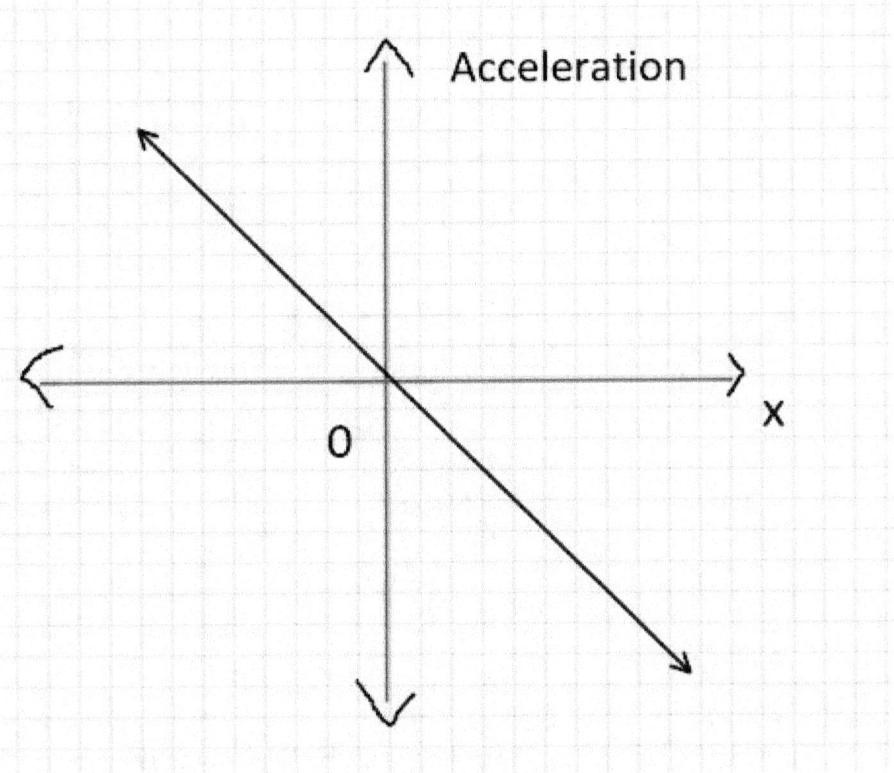

3. For v v/s x

When the particle does the SHM the particle is pulled by a conservative force in the opposite direction to the displacement of the particle. Therefore when the particle is moving in the -ve x direction, it will have a force positive which means an acceleration positive, due to the driving force, which again means a reducing velocity of the particle at the negative Amplitude '-A' ,and, the particle, when moves in the +ve direction of x will have a force negative, which means an acceleration negative, due the the driving force, meaning a velocity of the particle decreasing to zero on reaching to positive amplitude 'A'.The maxium velocity is always while crossing the mean position as the kinetic energy of the particle is maximum there.

Since the formula of v in a SHM is $v^2 = (\omega^2)(A^2 - x^2)$, therefore the graph of it is like this:

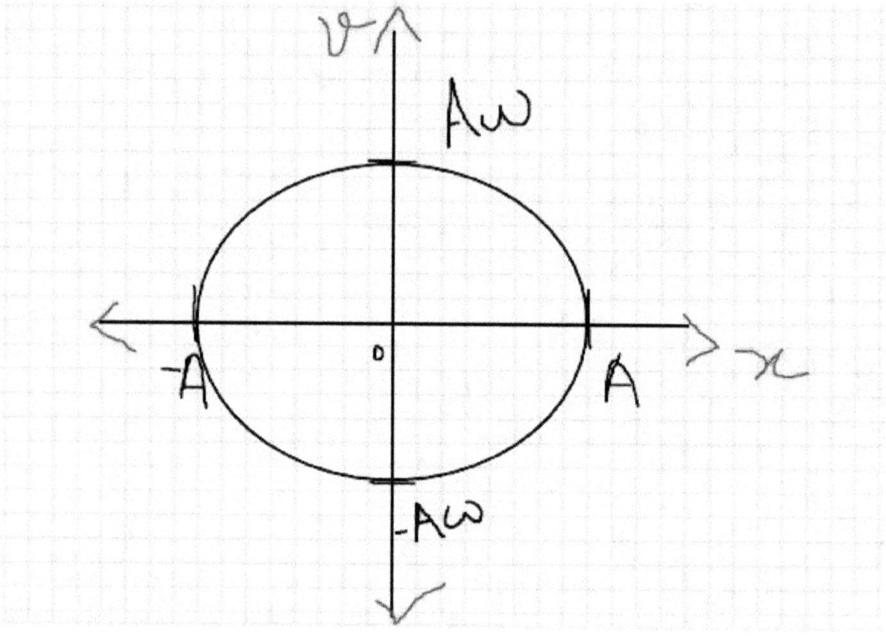

4. For x v/s t

As it is earlier derived that x is directly proportional to the sine function or cosine function of ωt. Therefore from this we understand that this x v/s t graph, would be a sinusodial or cosine wave because we have to represent a sine or cosine function on the graph. The graph is represented like this (the graph is for $x = A \sin\omega t$) :

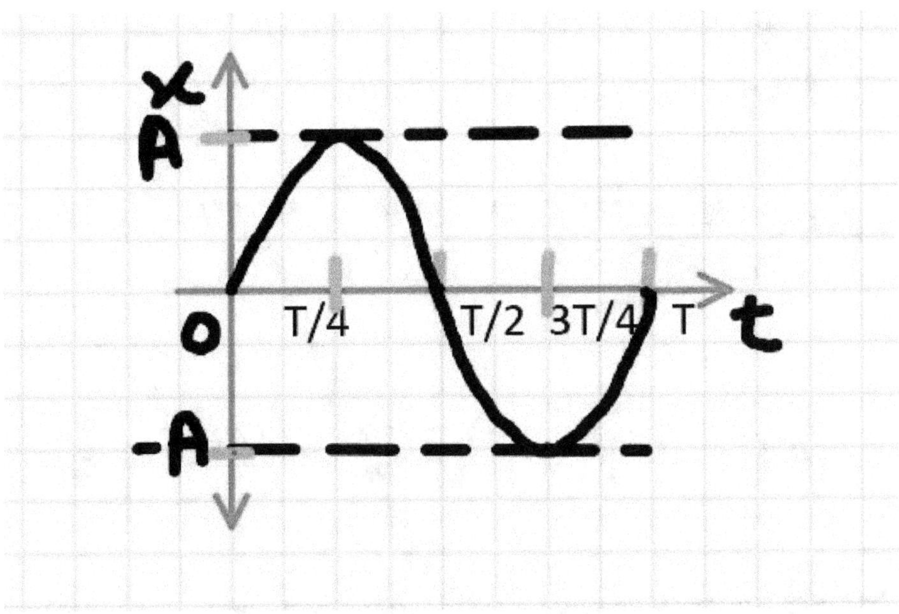

The graph for x= A cosωt is represented like this :

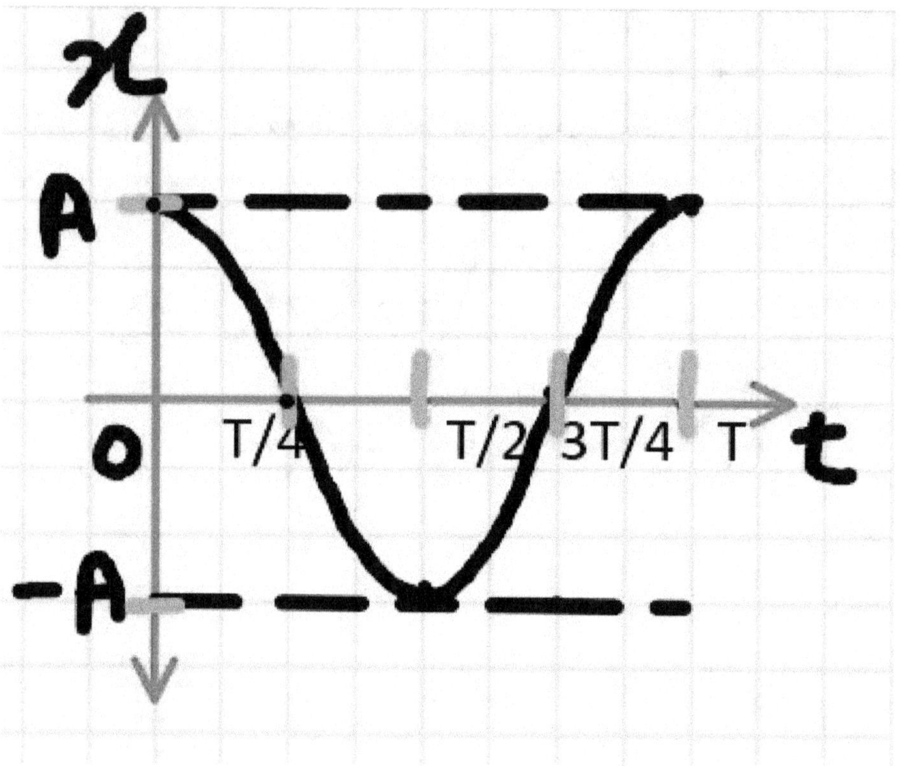

Here in the this cosine wave graph the particle at t=0 is at the amplitude because mathematically if put the value of t=0 in x= A cosωt, x becomes A which is the maximum value of x as cos(0) = 1.

5. For v v/s t

As it is earlier derived that v is directly proportional to the cosine function or the sine function of ωt . Therefore from this we understand that this v v/s t graph, would be a cosine or sine wave graph. The graph is represented like this (the graph is for v= A ω cosωt) :

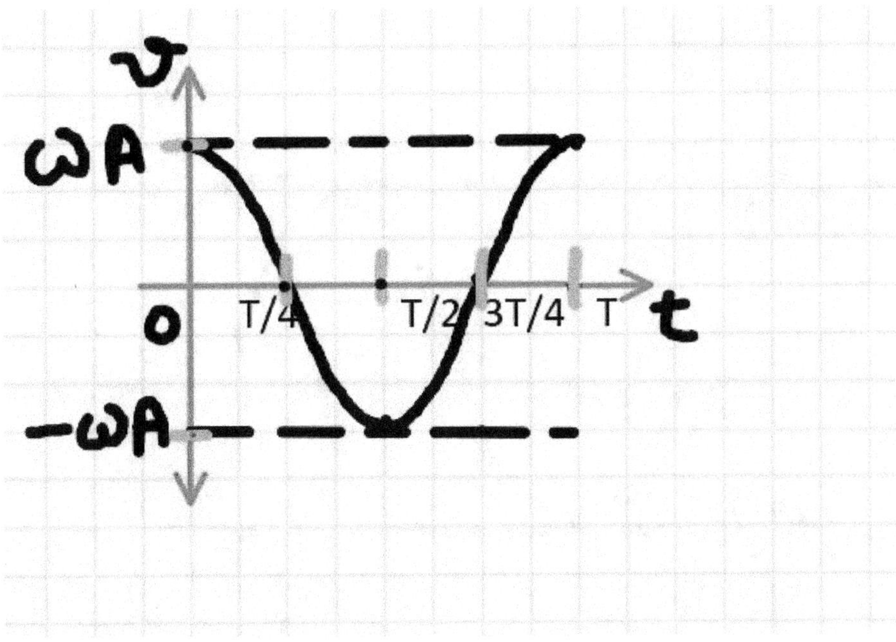

This shows that in the mean position the particle has the maximum velocity and in the amplitudes due to the act of the conservative force, the acceleration and velocity both decreases.

The graph for v= - A ω sinωt looks like this the following:

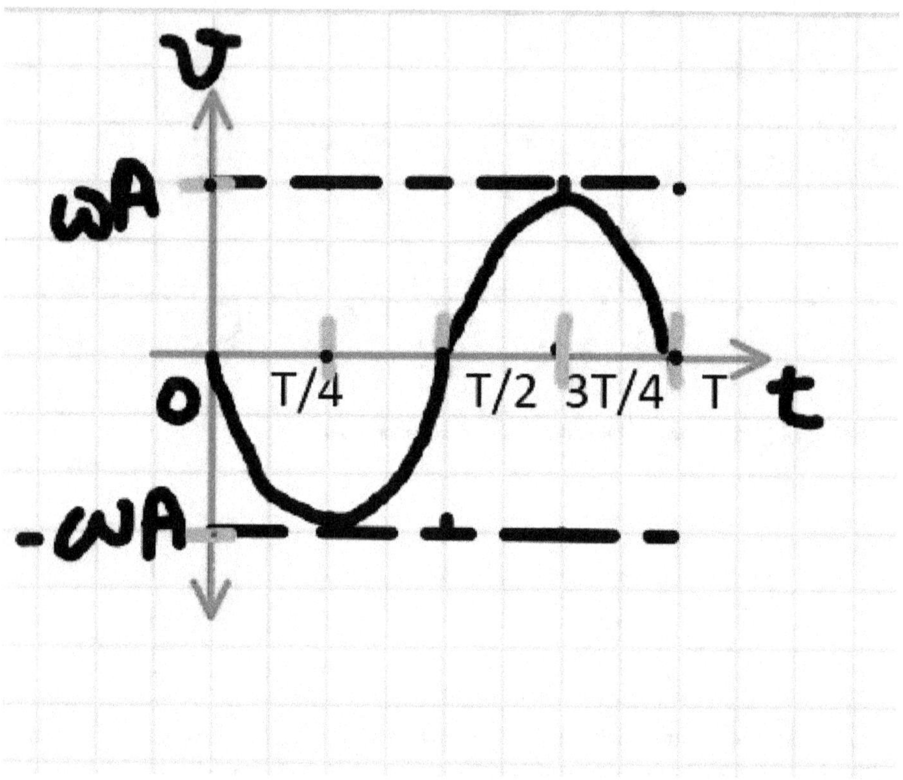

Since the formula for v, when the particle starts from the amplitude is v= -A ω sinωt, therefore the graph is like a sine wave and it starts being at the 4th quadrant(+,-) and then comes to the 1st quadrant (+,+). Henceforth, velocity vary in this manner in SHM.

6. For a v/s t

As it is earlier derived that a is directly proportional to the sine function or cosine function of ωt . Therefore from this we understand that this a v/ s t graph, would be a sine or cosine wave because we have to represent a sine or cosine function on the graph. The graph is represented like this (the graph is for a=-A(ω^2) sinωt) :

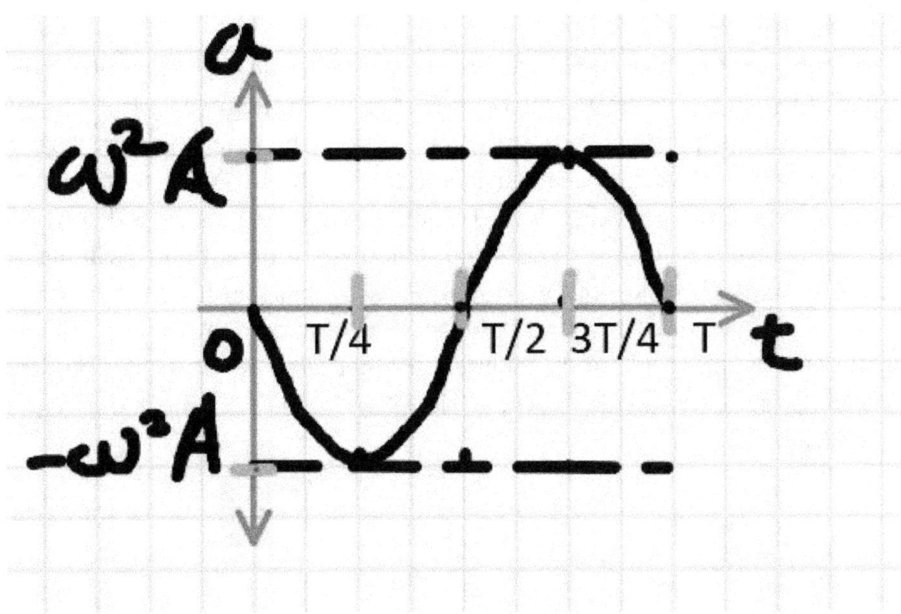

The graph for a= - A (ω^2) cosωt looks like this the following:

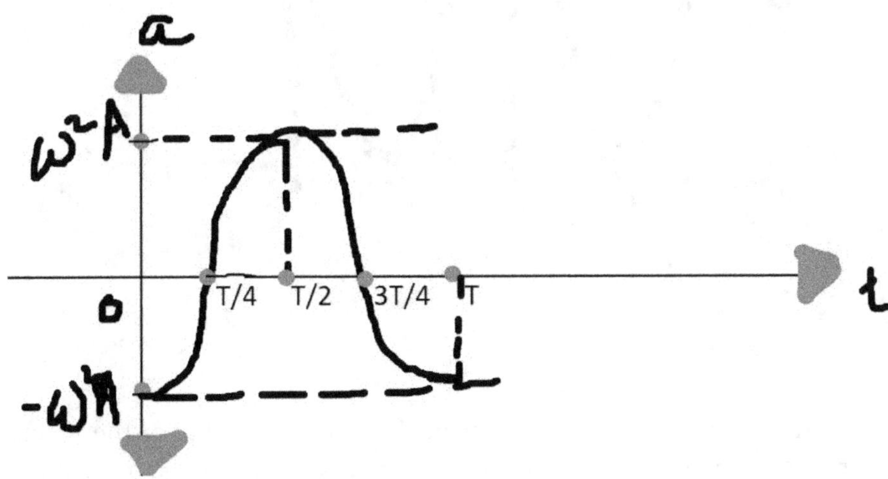

Therefore the acceleration also pscillates, in terms of values , like first it comes from the 1st quadrant(+,+), then goes to the 4th quadrant (+,-) and then again to the 1st quadrant and so on so forth.

7. For KE v/s t

When a particle in SHM moves from one amplitude to the amplitude on other of the mean position of it various changes in the mechanical energy take place in the particle. Here we will talk about the kinetic energy versus time graph where we have the consideration that the at t=0 the particle is at the mean position, meaning at x=0. Therefore when the particle is disturbed from the mean position , it starts the SHM. Therefore when it will again reach the mean position the maximum force will act on it and then more is the velocity of the object and so it will have maximum Kinetic energy at the centre and would and absolutely 0 kinetic energy at its amplitudes, according to the formula K.E. = (0.5) k [(A^2) - (x^2)]. See the graph below carefully:

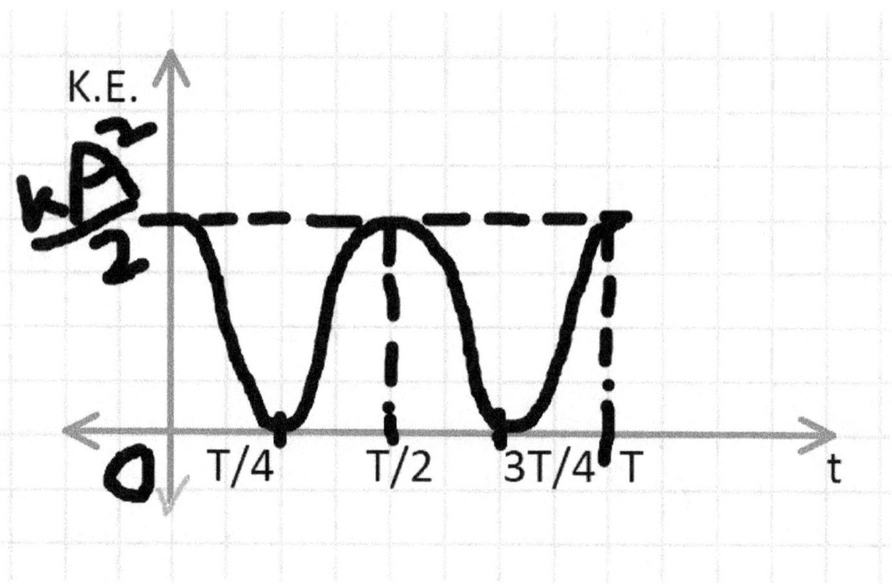

The thing here is to observe that in the graph the value of the K.E is never negative but only becomes 0, meaning that this is not an oscillating quantity which oscillates in both positve and negative values, just as the velocity , displacement etc. This also verifies that energy can neither be created nor be destroyed. In the SHM of a particle. We can even see the graph for the particle at x=a at t=0 time. It would be something like this:

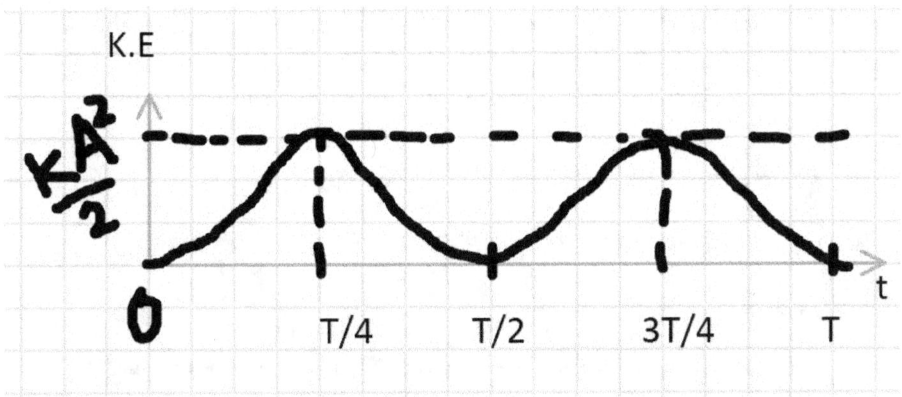

8. For PE v/s t

The potential energy of the particle keeps on changing, like at the mean position it is the mean posiition is the minimum or 0 sometimes and at the amplitudes it is the maximum, i.e. $(0.5)k(A^2)$. We will consider it as zero at the mean position for the sake of simplicity. There the graph of Potential of the particle in SHM versus the time is like the below, when it's at the mean position where x = 0 at time t = 0 , and the SHM starts :

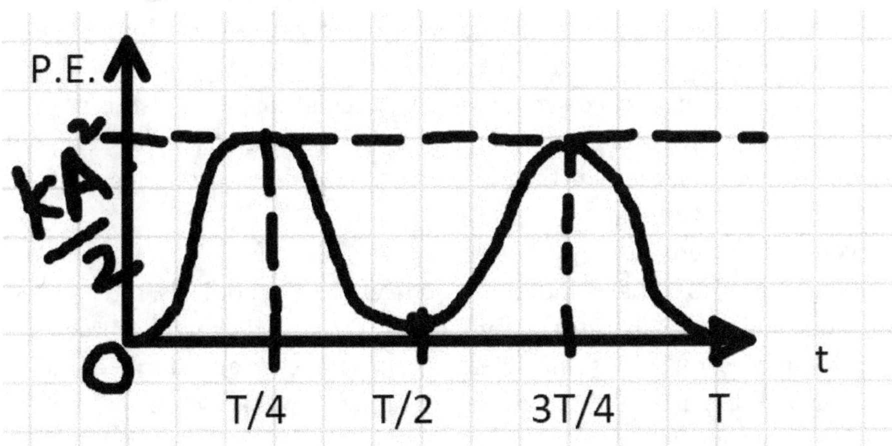

Just like the the graph of K.E. , the graph of P.E. also have no negative values as its energy (Potential energy) , here also the law of conservation of energy is maintained . On the other hand when the particle starts from the amplitude , meaning x= A at time t= 0 . It's graph changes like the below:

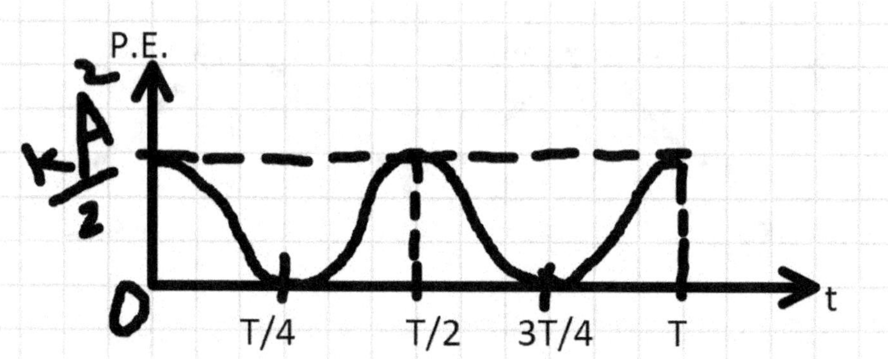

The Hollow Hole Through The Earth: A Hypothetical concept of SHM

- **An introduction to Hypothesis**

A **hypothesis** (plural hypotheses) is a proposed explanation for a phenomenon. For a hypothesis to be a scientific hypothesis, the scientific method requires that one can test it. Scientists generally base scientific hypotheses on previous observations that cannot satisfactorily be explained with the available scientific theories. Even though the words "hypothesis" and "theory" are often used synonymously, a scientific hypothesis is not the same as a scientific theory. A working hypothesis is a provisionally accepted hypothesis proposed for further research, in a process beginning with an educated guess or thought.

What is a Scientific Hypothesis?

People refer to a trial solution to a problem as a hypothesis, often called an "educated guess" because it provides a suggested outcome based on the evidence. However, some scientists reject the term "educated guess" as incorrect. Experimenters may test and reject several hypotheses before solving the problem.

According to Schick and Vaughn, researchers weighing up alternative hypotheses may take into consideration:

Testability (compare falsifiability as discussed above)

Parsimony (as in the application of "Occam's razor", discouraging the postulation of excessive numbers of entities)

Scope – the apparent application of the hypothesis to multiple cases of phenomena

Fruitfulness – the prospect that a hypothesis may explain further phenomena in the future

Conservatism – the degree of "fit" with existing recognized knowledge-systems.

- **The Hollow hole passing from the center of the earth**

The earth as we perceive today, is indeed very beautiful and of course who wants to make a hole on and through the earth? It's us . We will make holes through earth **hypothetically.** Just for the sake of basic knowledge acquiring purpose we will first make a hole through the centre of earth. Like this : (see fig.6)

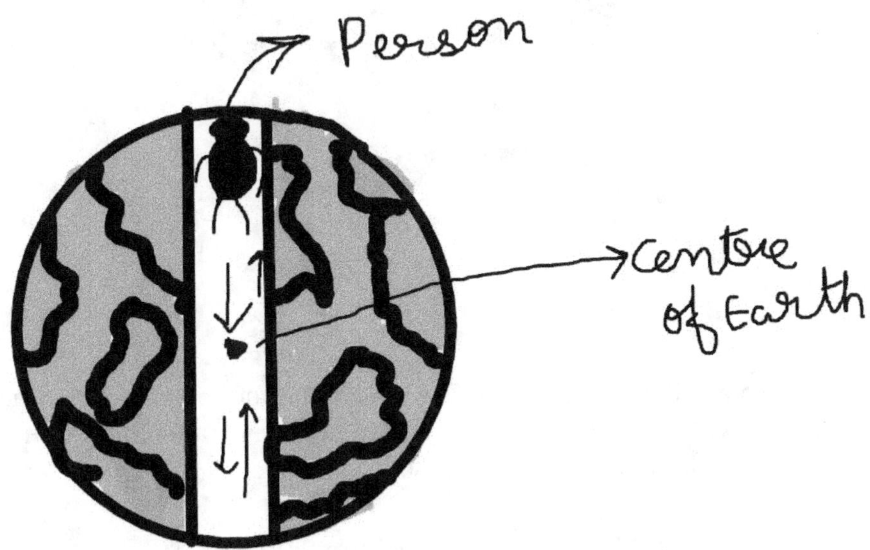

Fig.6 the person falling from the opening of hole through earth

Consider a person falling from the opening of the hole. The gravitational force pulls him/her towards the centre. So there is an SHM going on due to the gravity. For knowing it properly, let's calculate time period of the person in SHM under the action of the force of gravity.

We will use here the formula for g' = g (1-d/R) {derivation to be published in the next edition of Ask Physics, i.e. Ask Physics 4}, where g is the acceleration due to gravity on the surface of earth, the g' is the new acceleration due to gravity due to the decrease in the radius considered, and d is the following (See fig.7)

Fig.7 shows 'd' which is the measure of the distance of body under the action of gravity which is below the earth from the circumference of earth.

at the surface d=0 , so 1-0/R = 1, hence g' = g.

Thus, the representaion of the force acting on the body is :

F= -m*(g')

=> F = -m*(g(1-d/R))

=>F = -m*(g(R-d)/R))

=>F = -mgx/R................{considering x=R-d}

=> F= -kx..........{ where k=mg/R}

So now we need to find the time period of the SHM as we have confirmed that its an SHM by finding the measure of force as -kx, so we get the time period of the motion by the following,

k=mg/R is similar to k/m=a/x , and a=ω^2 x

putting a=ω^2 x

we get,

=>k/m = ω^2 x / x

=>k/m = ω^2

=>√(k/m) = ω...............(i)

we know,

ω=2π/T

or,

T= 2π/ω..............(ii)

putting value of ω from (i) in (ii)

we get,

T=2π(√(m/k))

=> T= 2π(√(mR/mg))...............................[k=mg/R]

=> T= 2π(√(R/g)) so we get the time period as this eqn.

So we can reach the bottom of the hole in approximately 81.46 minutes!!

- **The Hollow hole passing through any place on earth**

The descriptions given above are same . But now the case is not the same the diagram becomes like this now. (See fig. 8.)

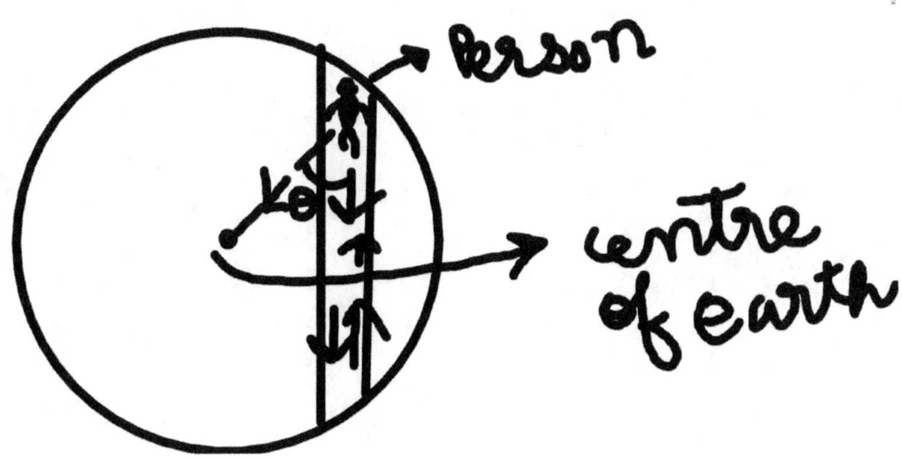

Fig.8 Showing a hole made at the place away from the centre and doesn't pass through the centre

Here the force's measure is the x axis component of the mg that's mgcosθ and since its an SHM,

F=-kxcosθ

but the time period has no influence of cosθ and hence θ. So the time period is that same 81.46 minutes.It is just that the force applied by the centre of the earth and the freuency of the oscillation would decrease becaus e here not the direct force, but the component of it is acting.

CHAPTER ELEVEN

Mechanical Waves-1

Imagine that you have an ideal string at a fixed end. You see that the wave in the rope gets reflected back from the fixed end. You can even imagine of a bucket having still water where in you put one drop of water at the centre of the circle (not neccesarily needed to be the centre, but just for an ideal observation). You see a wave propagation. Actually, the waves which are formed on the water surface comprises of two waves in two different direction with respect to the direct of the propagation of the Disturbance or the Energy, one is the capillary wave and the other is the gravity wave formed after the drop hits the surface and the there is depression created on the surface of water, the water bumps upwards due to its surface tension and then, again gravity pulls it downwards, and in this way the disturbance propagates further; then comes the capillary waves which forms when the depression is created and the molecules is pulled forward due to the forces of attraction between them, this causes this longitudinal wave to propagate further as a series of the to and fro motion of the particles of the water, see Fig. 1 and Fig.2:

Fig.1 Before the water drop hits the surface

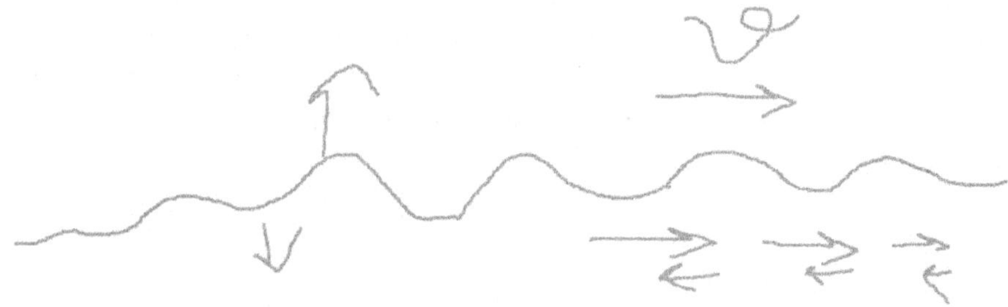

Fig.2 After the water drop hit the placed, and caused both Capillary
waves and Gravity waves

Note that in a wave motion only and only the Disturbance or the Energy
of the disturbance applied or created travels not the particle in SHM. The
particles carrying the disturbance just oscillate about their mean position
but they don't actually move vertically rather than oscillating about their

mean position, except the disturbance in the wave motion.

Everytime in our life we see light performing different phenomena, we even hear sound, as well as we even speak, sometimes loudly and sometimes not. But what is this sound and light. They are Waves. Waves are basically result of some disturbances caused due to vibrations of body. The body vibrates at different rates, to perform different kinds of Frequencies. Waves based on two criterions can be divided into two types:

i) On the basis of the medium

1. Mechanical Wave

The waves which need a medium to travel is called as a Mechanical wave. They cannot traverse in a medium-less environment. Its examples contain sound waves, waves on a string, capillary waves etc.

This the topic which is to be discussed in this chapter.

2. Non-mechanical Waves

The waves which do not require a medium are called Non-Mechanical waves. They can also traverse through medium but their respective speeds are reduced more, when the density of the medium is more. Its examples include UV(Ultraviolet) light , IR(Infra-Red) light, Cosmic rays etc. In a whole we can tell that all the electromagnetic waves are non-mechanical waves.

This topic is to be discussed in the in the chapters of the upcoming books.

ii) On the basis of the movement wave with respect to the direction of the wave propagation

1. Transverse Waves

In these waves the oscillations are perpendicular to the direction of wave propagtion. Take the example of the waves on a cloth when we shake it roughly and give it a pulse in the horizontal direction. The cloth due to the pulse behaves like a transverse wave , and the thing to observe was that, the disturbance in the cloth created by us, travels perpendicular to the wave formation direction. For other examples we have waves on a string, electromagnetic waves, gravity waves on a water surface etc.

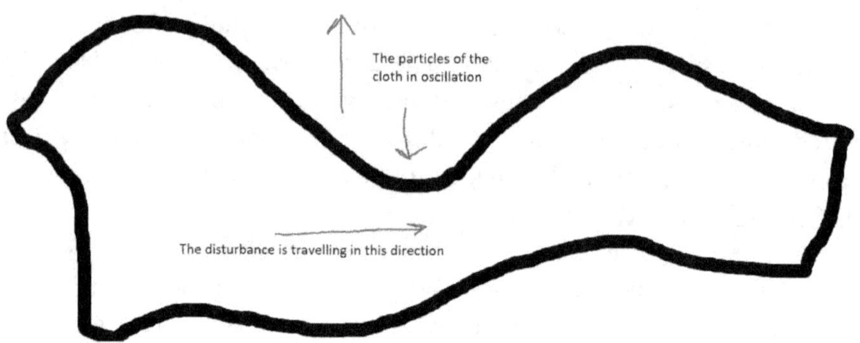

The above figure shows us how the cloth behaves when we give it a rapid pulse.

2. Longitudinal waves

The waves have their disturbances travelling in the direction of the wave propagation. Thus, the disturbances in their wave motion are parallel to the direction of wave propagation. The wave motion in this case travels in a continuos series of motion in the material medium. This motion is divided into two parts : rarefaction and compression. **Rarefaction** is the expansion of the space between the particles in the material medium when they gain kinetic energy from the force applied on them, which then lead to the simple harmonic motion of the particle after they collide with the particles at resting at a distance. and then gives some energy to the particle, earlier at rest, and then comes back . This coming back of the particle and the contraction of space between them is called as **Compression**. This chain of motion goes on, until and unless the the energy in the particle is not sufficient for disturbing the particle resting or the energy is not enough for reaching the particle at rest. This is why sound fades in gases more quickly than in liquids and fades quickly in comparison to solids in liquids. More precisely, **Rarefaction** is the region of low pressure and density created when the particles which were earlier set into motion comes back after hitting the layer of particles infront of them. On the other hand, **Compression** is that region where there is high pressure and density. This region is formed when the particles are just hit by the particles which were set into motion earlier. The sequence of the motion continues as Compression then Rarefaction, again Compression then again Rarefaction and so on and so forth.

Further the example given in the transversal wave for the pulse in a cloth also produces a sound wave if the pulse is high. The thing that happens is that the cloth hits the column of air present below it with an amount of force which decides the intensity, of the sound wave. Thus sound wave and capillary waves are ideal examples for this category of waves.

Displacement Relation in a Progressive wave

Let the source of the wave be situated at the origin of the axis. We see that the wave so produced progresses along the x axis and grows and deepens repeatedly in the y axis and as the amplitude of each particle in the wave depends on the position of the particle and the time for which we are talking about .

We require the x axis position of the particle and the time we are dealing with, so, the y(x,t) is position of the particle w.r.t. to y axis is the quantity we require to find of the particle which is also the perpendicular displacement of the wave at the point of x and t . Thus y(x,t) is defined for all x and t. Now, lets find the displacement of this plane progressive wave so travelling.

So first we consider a graph below. According to the graph we'll get the y(x,t) of the wave.

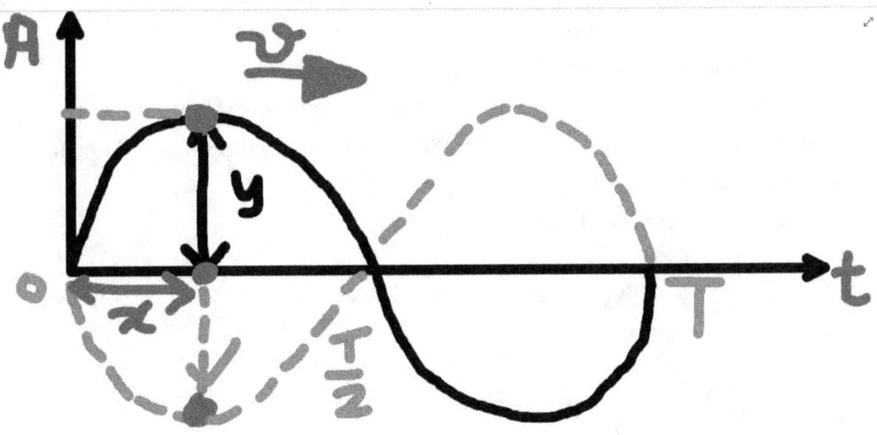

The particle's disturbance moves throughout the wave motion caused due to the source at t-x/v where t is the time of the particle's position we are referring to, but, the particle at x=0 or at source is the particle which is associated with the t-x/v term.

So ,

the y (particle after t time at x distance from the origin) = y(particle at the origin in t-x/v time)

And because its SHM, so,

$y(x,t) = A \sin (\omega(t-x/v) + \Phi)$

$\Rightarrow y(x,t) = A \sin (\omega t-\omega x/v + \Phi)$

$\Rightarrow y(x,t) = A \sin (\omega t - kx + \Phi)$

Thus , the above is the general equation for the waves (plane progressive waves), where '$(\omega t - kx + \Phi)$' is the phase of the particle and A is the amplitude of the particle.

Leaving the intial phase we get another form of this equation; i.e. :

$y(x,t) = A \sin 2\pi[(t/T) \pm (x/\lambda)]$.....taking 2π common from bot ωt and kx

.

We should also know about the general form of a wave equation that is:

$y = f(ax \pm bt)$

where we specify y of the wave to be a function totally dependent on x and t and a and b are the coefficients of x and t respectively.

we also define a quantity in a differential form:

$\partial(\partial y/(\partial t))/\partial t = K(\partial(\partial y/\partial x)/\partial x)$

where K is a constant and y is double differentiated w.r.t to t and x on L.H.S and R.H.S respectively.

Speed of the Travelling Wave

We know that the speed of any thing is the change in its position per unit time or $\Delta x/\Delta t$. So kx becomes $k(x+\Delta x)$ and ωt becomes $\omega(t+\Delta t)$,then on equating them we get,

$kx - \omega t = k(x+\Delta x) - \omega(t+\Delta t)$

$\Rightarrow kx - \omega t = k(x+\Delta x) - \omega(t+\Delta t)$

$\Rightarrow kx - \omega t = kx + k\Delta x - \omega t - \omega\Delta t$

$\Rightarrow k\Delta x - \omega\Delta t = 0$

$\Rightarrow k\Delta x = \omega\Delta t$

$\Rightarrow \Delta x / \Delta t = \omega / k$

$\Rightarrow v = \omega / k$

or,

$v = 2\pi v/2\pi/\lambda$

$\Rightarrow v = v \lambda$, where λ is wavelength of the wave and v is the frequency of the wave.

This is a general equation for velocity of all progressive wave.

But,

The waves like sound and that on a string have other factor to be put in consideration like bulk modulus of the medium [to be discussed in upcoming books] of wave propagation, Tension of the string , Density of the medium of wave propagation etc.

Now we obtain the velocity expression for the wave in a string,

Observe the graph in (a) and the diagram (b).

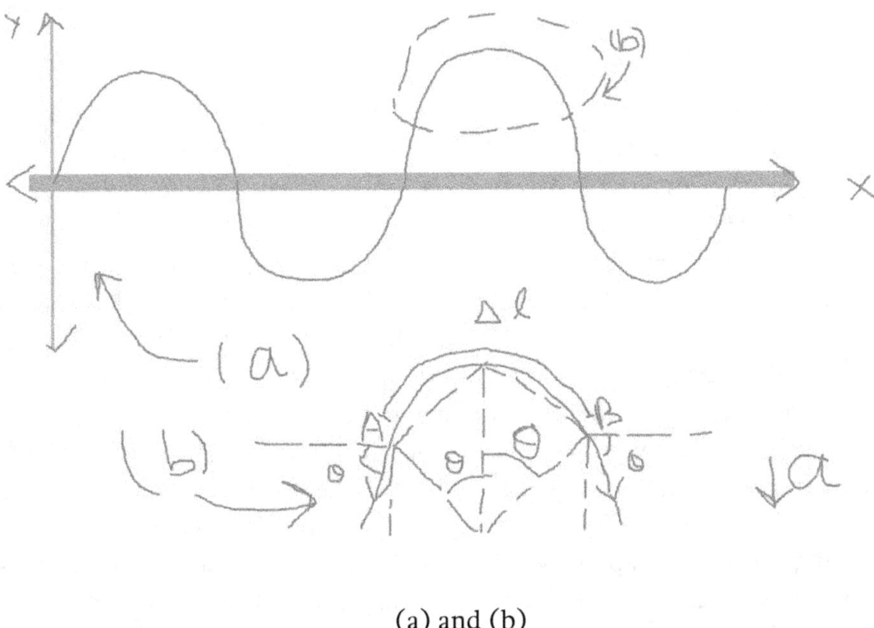

(a) and (b)

As we see the (b) figure we see that on the either sides the tension is acting on the strings so as the net acceleration of the string's wave's crest is downwards, so taking the y axis components of force of tension we get,

$F = F\sin\theta + F\sin\theta$

$F = 2F\sin\theta$

and we can tell the approximate value of $\sin\theta$ i.e.

$\sin\theta \approx [\Delta l/2]/R$

putting this value in $F = 2F\sin\theta$

we get,

$F = F\Delta l/R$

and as F= mv/t

we obtain,

mv/t = FΔl/R

and so we obtain,

v = FΔlt/mR

as R/t is velocity (v) and m/Δl is 'μ' or linear mass density,

v= F/vμ

or,

v^2 = F/μ

or,

v = $\sqrt{(F/\mu)}$

where v is the velocity of the wave on the string , F is the tension and μ is the linear mass density.

The linear mass density of a string having density ρ, diameter d is:

μ = π(d^2)ρ / 4

We are now supposed to find the velocity of sound wave, so we first we have to know about the behavior of the sound wave. Its basically a disturbance caused in the material, i.e the three states of matter that are solid, liquid and gas. Its produced by a vibrating source. The particles here, due to the disturbance move parallely in the direction of wave propagation and thus cause difference or oscillations in their displacement, pressure and density as well. In other cases, like of light there are variations in the E & B fields causing the wave and are also perpendicular to each other. Keeping those cases apart, we move with sound waves for now and thus give an ideal example from this i.e. of a tuning fork. The tuning fork is first hit at surface for involving the prongs in the production of sound waves, thus acting as a vibration source. The prongs, when vibrates, due to the force exterted by the surface, goes towards each other, and then due to the material tension, it comes back again, going farther from each other. This causes a pulse in the material medium present around it, and thus gets compressed, this compression leads to increments in density of the medium and the pressure in the medium around the prongs. Due to this pressure the particles of the medium collide further (compression), keeping some energy with themselves and some given to the particles forwards. So, this forms a gap. This series of compression and rarefaction carries on untill and unless the net kinetic energy becomes zero for the particles so propagated. Hence gets damped.

However, the tuning fork produces a compression pulse of length vT/2 ans it happens during the half time period of the SHM of the prongs. Another half period of Timeperiod is spent on the rarefaction pulse where the prongs comes backwards and thus the material medium around it expands. See the following graph and the diagram . See Fig. (a) & (b).

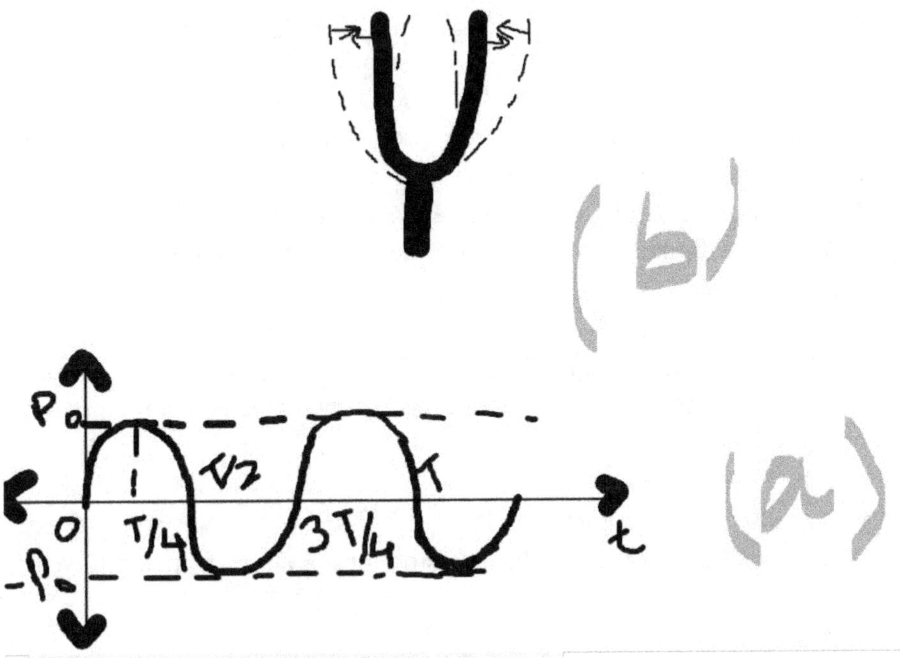

(a) graph of Po variations and (b) is the tuning fork

Since the pressure variations in the sound wave forms a sine wave, hence, we also observe a simple harmonic type of variation as the rate of change of Pressure variations depend on the angular frequency of the sound wave, so, we get the result of it as:

$\delta P = P - Po = \delta Po \sin\omega t$

$\Rightarrow \delta P = \delta Po \sin\omega t$

$\Rightarrow \delta P = \delta Po \sin\omega(t - x/v)$------------For the sound wave's pressure variance when the sound waves progresses on the x axis with time. Here, δP is the change in the pressure observed and δPo is the maximum change in pressure that can be observed.

we can also write it as the following:

p= po sinω(t-x/v), where p is excess or deficit pressure observed and po is the maximum pressure that can be obtained than the normal one.

Now we shall also focus on the dispalcement of the particle that's s .

so since it varies harmonically, so ,

s=so sinω(t-x/v)

=> Δs = -[ω so /v] cos ω(t-x/v) Δx.....(derivating w.r.t. x and here so is 's not' which is the max. value of s to be obtained)

Now, we visualize the wave motion, we observe a change in the position x, which becomes x+Δx , that cause the displacement of the wave to increase from s to s+Δs, as the waves progress the position of the points are displaced by the amounts of s and s+Δs repectively and the cross section of the wave gives a cross sectional area A and cause the change in volume to be:

ΔV= AΔs

ΔV/V = -[A [ω so /v] cos ω(t-x/v) Δx]/ [A Δx]

=>ΔV/V = - [ω so /v] cos ω(t-x/v)

and the bulk modulus of the medium is B which means that the pressure should also be:

P = B(-ΔV/V)

=> P = B [ω so /v] cos ω(t-x/v)

and for the max. value of P that's Po and for cos ω(t-x/v) that's 1, we get ;

Po= B ω so /v = B k so

Again now we take out the force acting on the Area A to be pA and to be (p+Δp)A

so,

ΔF = -AΔp

=> ΔF = -A [po ω/ v] sin ω(t-x/v)Δx

=>ΔF = -A (B ω so /v) (ω/ v) sin ω(t-x/v)Δx

=>ΔF = -A (B (ω^2) so / (v^2)) sin ω(t-x/v)Δx

also acceleration in the system (wave) is:

a= ΔF / ρ A Δx

=> a = -A (B (ω^2) so / (v^2)) sin ω(t-x/v)Δx/ ρ A Δx

=> a = -B (ω^2) s /ρ(v^2)............(i)

and even we can take out acceleration of the system (wave) by ,

a= ∂(∂s/∂t)/∂t

a= -(ω^2)s...............(ii)

Equating both (i) and (ii)

$-(\omega^2)s = -B(\omega^2)s/\rho(v^2)$

$\Rightarrow B = \rho(v^2)$

$\Rightarrow v = \sqrt{(B/\rho)}$

Similarly, in solids we consider Y that's Young Modulus.

and $v = \sqrt{(Y/\rho)}$

The story of Laplace correction

The formula of Speed of sound in gas was also given by Sir Issac Newton, where he considered PV=constant, and thus concluded that the temperature changes are neglible as they take place during the wave motion of sound waves. Hence he considered the process to be isothermal and thus suggested that ;

$v = \sqrt{(P/\rho)}$

But, then came Laplace and he corrected the value of velocity to be $v = \sqrt{(\gamma P/\rho)}$ where γ is the constant for a given gas and is in fact said to be the ratio of the two specific heat capacities $\gamma = Cp/Cv$ [To be discussed in the upcoming books]. He said that the propagation of Sound waves is an adiabatic process because they do get compressed and rarefied and thus exchanges energy in the form of work and not heat. Thus the value of the velocity of sound was now calculated to be 332 m/s at STP(Standard temperature and pressure)

Principle of Superposition of Waves

When two or more waves traverse in the same medium the net displacement of the superposing waves is given by the algebraic sum of the two or more waves . This is known as the principle of superposition of the waves.

Thus,

$y(x,t) = \Sigma$ fi $(x - vt)$, where i is initiated with 1 and is limited by the no. n.(where $n \in N$)

For the sake of simplicity, we will work with the two waves superposing with each other with their amplitudes same as each other, i.e. A and having all the values same for k, x, t, and ω but are separted by Φ phase difference from each other. Let their displacements be y. for the first and y.. for the second with phase Φ.

The principle of superposition of waves tells us that :

y net = y. + y..

$\Rightarrow$ y net = a sin (kx - ωt) + a sin (kx - ωt + Φ)

=> y net = a (sin (kx - ωt) + sin (kx - ωt + Φ))

=> y net = 2 a cos(Φ/2) sin (kx - ωt + Φ/2)

So this the equation of the resultant wave so formed by the superposition of the two waves but this not the only equation if there are more than three waves we get a different expression and so on, so forth.

For constructive interference of the waves we get $\Phi = 0$, 2π, 4π, 6π ....

For destructive interference of the waves we get $\Phi = \pi$, 3π, 5π, 7π ....

CHAPTER TWELVE

Some Wave Phenomena-1

Reflection of Waves

The Waves are nothing but the Disturbance which travel in the medium whether it be any of the media, a solid, liquid and gas. This is valid for mechanical waves as well as non-mechanical waves. The only difference would be that the mechanical waves would be created if this disturbance flows through a material medium, and for the non-mechanical waves, the disturbance can travel in vacuum, where there's no medium.

At the primary level, these disturbances in particles of the medium, when hit an end to which they are confined to, and according to 3rd law of motion gets pushed back and is thus reflected backwards. These reflection varies in certain ways mentioned below. Here we consider a string tied to a fixed end.

• Reflection from a fixed end

The string is fixed to fixed end and is provided a pulse creating a crest which then progresses and reflects back to the source in the form of a trough as the fixed end provides a rigidity to the wave in the string and so the last particle reaching the amplitude a now reaches the amplitude -a . As it gets a chance to continue its SHM. So the reflected wave is separated from the incident wave by π rad. phase. So the equation of displacement for the wave produced from the source is,

$y(x,t) = a \sin(\omega t - kx)$

And that for the reflected wave is ,

$y(x,t) = a \sin(\omega t + kx + \pi) = -a \sin(\omega t + kx)$

So net Resultant wave is zero as on superposing they cancel out, if imagined as two seperate pulses coming towards each other.

• __Reflection from a free end__

The string is fixed to free end and is provided a pulse creating a crest which then progresses and reflects back to the source in the form of the same crest the source produced earlier as the end now allows the last particle of the string to oscillate reaching the same amplitude a as produced ealier . It gets a chance to continue its SHM. So the refleced wave is seperated from the incident wave by 0 rad. phase . So the equation of displacement for the wave produced from the source is ,

$y(x,t) = a \sin(\omega t - kx)$

And that for the reflected wave is ,

$y(x,t) = a \sin(\omega t + kx)$

So net Resultant produces twice the no. of Amplitude a i.e. 2a as on superposing they now don't cancel out, if imagined as two seperate pulses coming towards each other and gets added to each other

$y \text{ net} = a\,[\sin(\omega t - kx) + \sin(\omega t + kx)]$

$\Rightarrow y \text{ net} = 2\,a \sin(\omega t) \cos(kx)$

• __Reflection and transmission of waves in a heavy-light string system__

Sometimes it happens that when a light string is connected to heavier string or such an end which is not totally fixed not totally free. This type of case cause a disturbance on both the heavy string in the form of transmission and in the light string in the form of reflection with a phase π rad. between the pulse and the reflected wave.

Let us consider a case where we have two string where one has a linear mass density bigger than that of the other. Let us name the heavier one as B and the lighter one as A. So when A is given a pulse it reaches the junction of the joining of the two strings where it gets both reflected and transmitted as a light ray/beam does, when it gets incidented on a transparent glass slab after refracting and reflecting from the surface. Now when the case is inverted we observe that when a pulse is provided to the heavy string it does the same phenomena, where it gets reflected and transmitted both at the same time. But this time it gets reflected with a 0 rad. phase in between the pulse and the reflected wave. See fig. 1.

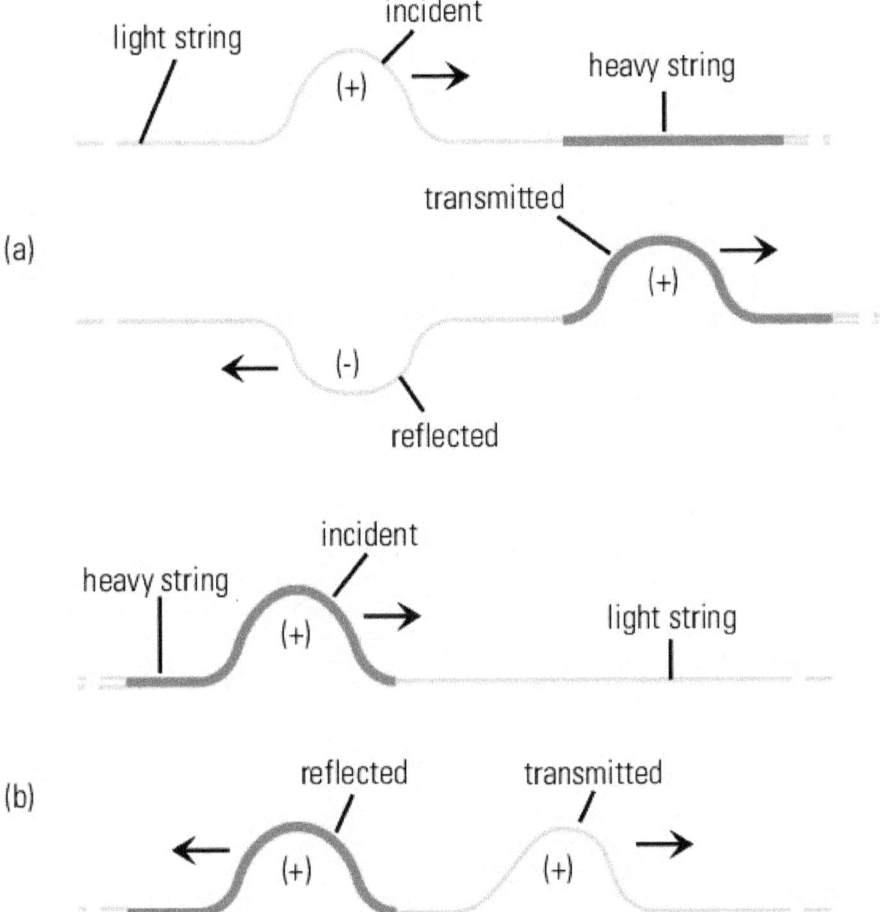

Fig.1-- Showing the reflection and transmission of waves in a heavy-light string system, in (a) is showing the reflection and transmission of waves on the light-heavy string system and (b) is showing the heavy-light string system's reflection and transmission of waves. We also observe that due to the high mass density of the heavy string the transmission of wave is having lesser amplitude in magnitude in comparison to the magnitude of amplitude of the reflected wave as $v = \sqrt{(F/\mu)}$ and $v \propto 1/\sqrt{(\mu)}$ also we observe that the reflected wave in (b) is having lesser amplitude in magnitude than that of the transmitted wave.The main trick of understanding it is imagining the phenomena.

- **<u>Stationary waves in a string fixed in both the ends</u>**

The waves that remain at a fixed position and perform SHM particle by particle and are thus confined under a particular area and there is no propagation of it due to fixed ends and also faces the reflection of the same , is named as stationary waves. They can be obtained in many ways. Even in our ovens we confine the microwaves in a particular area to exchange energy with the food and thus are stationary waves themselves. Examples of them also includes the stringed instruments we play, like guitar, sitar, veena etc.

Lets consider an ideal case of a string tied to both ends of two brick and is vibrating with frequency $v.$, $v..,$ $v...$. And, it has wavelengths of $\lambda.$, $\lambda..$, $\lambda...$ in each three cases respectively.

So for the first we consider the wavelength to be $\lambda.$ and frequency to be $v.$ and the velocity of the wave motion is $v=\sqrt{(F/\mu)}$ where F is the tension of the string and μ is the linear mass density of the string .

we get ,

$v. = (1/\lambda.) (\sqrt{(F/\mu)})$

and also as $\Phi=kx=(2\pi/\lambda.)x = 2\pi n$

so,

$x= n\lambda.$, where n is 1,2,3,4,5..................

so,

$x = n \lambda. = l$

and ,

$l = n (2l)..............[\because \lambda.=l/2]$

$n=1/2$

Now,

$\lambda. = x / (n)$

$\lambda. = l / (n)..............[as\ x= l]$

$\lambda. =2\,l$

Also λ for all cases, it should be in the form of $2\,l\,/n$ where n is a natural no. .

This is called as the fundamental mode or the first mode of vibration.

Hence,

We also get

v. = v/ 2l. <--------------This called as the first harmonic or the fundamental frequency

The second mode of vibration consists of the following things:

First we have λ.. = l

As, λ = 2l/n

And n here is 2, so we get the result mentioned above.

As λ..=l=v/v..

So, v.. = v/l

This called the first overtone and also the second harmonic.

Again, third mode of vibration consists of the following things:

As, here n= 3, so,

λ... = 2l/3= v/v...

v... = 3v/2l

This is again called as the second overtone or the third harmonic.

The position of the nodes and antinodes can be expressed as the following:

As the nodes lie where there is 0 amplitude and antinodes lie where there is maximum amplitude of the stationary waves so formed,hence we conclude that nodes should lie at x= 0, λ/2 , λ , 3λ/2 ....nλ/2 , (where n=1,2,3,4....) and the antinodes should lie at x = λ/4 , 3λ/4 , 5λ/4 ....(2n+1)λ/4 (where n=1,2,3,4........) .

Also, for nodes the positions are x= 0, l/n, 2l/n, 3l/n........Nl/n , where N is the no. of node and is subset of whole no. and n is the no. of harmonic.

And, for antinodes the positions are x= l/2n , 3l/2n, 5l/2n .... (2n-1)l/2n where n=1,2,3.......

We shall remember that the expression (n-1)l/2n, where n is 1,2,3,4........ so that when the value of this expression is 0,l/3,2l/5.... we get a node as here the no. of harmonics are increasing and when the values are l/4, 3l/8 ..... we get an antinode and we shall remember that this only valid for increasing no. of harmonics. See fig 2.

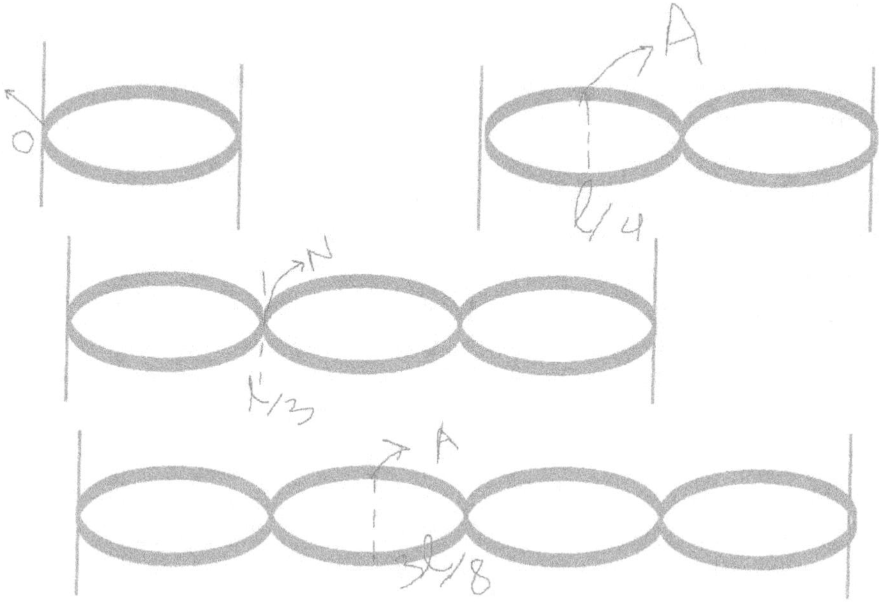

Fig.2 here A denotes Antinode and N denotes Node. Carefully observe this progression, also, here the first one is the diagram of the first harmonic, the next is of the second harmonic, its next is the third harmonic and the last is of fourth harmonic.

The natural frequency of the stationary waves of any harmonics are governed **$v = v/\lambda = nv/2l$, where n=1,2,3.....**

- ## <u>Standing waves and normal modes</u>

Standing waves are formed when there is no net movement or progression of the wave in a system so produced they are fixed in a certain area , have a particlular frequency and wavelength and velocity uptill a particular time and then due to damping effects it gets damped and diminished. Sometimes, due to multiple reflections, the waves get interfered and thus superposes with each other.

So because they come from opposite directions so considering them as ,

$y. = A \sin(\omega t - kx)$

and the reflected wave to be ,

y.. = A sin(ωt + kx)

Applying Principle of Superposition , we get,

y resultant = y. + y..

=> y resultant = A sin(ωt - kx) + A sin(ωt + kx)

=> y resultant = A [sin(ωt - kx) + sin(ωt + kx)]

=> **y resultant = 2A sin(ωt) cos(kx)**

Also as stated earlier,

We get nodes at x= 0, $\lambda/2$, λ , $3\lambda/2$, 2λ......$n\lambda/2$, (where n=1,2,3,4....) and the antinodes at x = $\lambda/4$, $3\lambda/4$, $5\lambda/4$, $7\lambda/4$ ....$(2n+1)\lambda/4$ (where n=1,2,3,4.......) and kx for nodes should be kx = 0, π, 2π, 3π, 4π .... $n\pi$, and for antinodes the kx should be kx = $\pi/2$, $3\pi/2$, $5\pi/2$, $7\pi/2$ .... $n\pi/2$ where n is odd and natural no. and this can be also expressed as $(n+1/2)\pi$.

Normal modes of vibration (frequency) is said to be that frequency which is also the natural frequency of the object in which it vibrates. The above values of x and kx, can be used to calculate the natural frequency of the string.

- <u>**Standing waves in the organ pipe**</u>

The waves created in an organ pipe is a stationary waves. Hence they would also follow the same condition as waves on a string on a fixed end and on a free end, though the equations are not so similar. Here we consider namely two cases, those are :

- <u>**Closed organ pipe**</u>

Closed organ pipe have one closed end and one open, so when a pulse of sound wave is produced they behave as the string and the fixed end reflection's case thus gets reflected from the end B if the pulse is produced in end A. See fig 3.

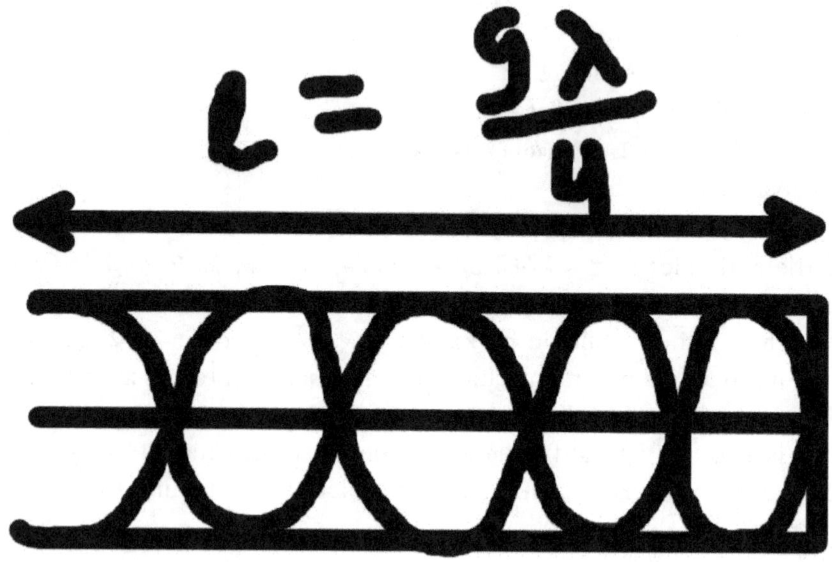

Fig. 3--Shows the closed organ pipe's reflection of sound phenomena, from A the sound pulse is produced and from B the sound is reflected. The waves (incident and reflected wave) have a phase difference of π radians.

Since it has one end open and one closed we get, $l = 9\lambda/4$, here in this case, so we can say that the first harmonic occurs when there are two nodes and one antinode is formed in a stationary wave, so here as we can see the sound waves propagates from A to B, we see that just at the starting we get an antinode and at the end we get a node so as no. of nodes here in this case is 4 we get $l = x = (2(4) + 1)\lambda/4 = 9\lambda/4$, so we thus conclude that $x = (2n+1)\lambda/4$, so all the nodes and antinodes can be represented in the form of the multiple of $(2n+1)/4$, and so the position of antinodes as discussed in 'Stationary waves in a string fixed in both the ends' topic are:

$x = \lambda/4$, $3\lambda/4$, $5\lambda/4$, $7\lambda/4$............**and so on.**

and for the position of nodes here the x becomes:

$x = 0, \lambda/2$, λ , $3\lambda/2, 2\lambda$...............**and so on.**

The frequency of the wave here is:

$v = (2n+1)v/4l$

and the wavelength of the stationary waves is:

$\lambda = 4l/(2n + 1)$

Ratio of the overtones = 3:5:7:9:11.......all odd nos. from 3 to ∞

- ## <u>Open organ pipe</u>

Open organ pipe have both ends open. So when a pulse of sound wave is produced they behave as the string and the free end reflection's case thus gets reflected from the end B if the pulse is produced in end A. See fig 4.

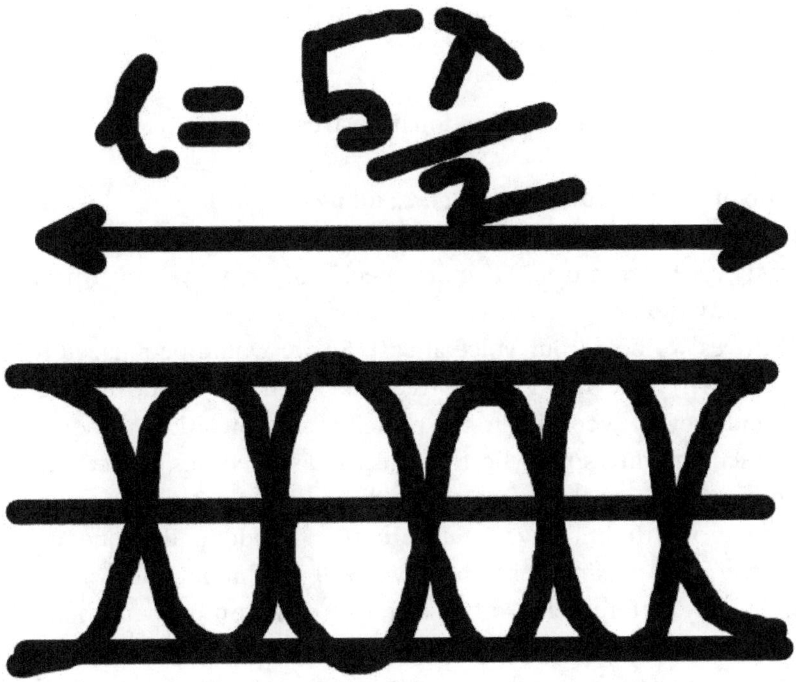

Fig. 4 shows the closed organ pipe's reflection of sound phenomena, From A the sound pulse is produced and from B the sound is reflected. The waves (incident and reflected wave) have a phase difference of 0 radians here.

Because it has both ends open, we get, $l = 5\lambda/2$, here in this case too, we can say that the first harmonic occurs when there is two nodes and one antinode is formed in the stationary wave present here, in this pipe, so here as we can see the sound waves propagates from A to B, we see that just at the starting we get an antinode and at the end we get an antinode so as no. of nodes here in this case is 5 we get,

$l = x = 10\lambda/4 = 5\lambda/2$

So we thus conclude that $x = n\lambda/4$, so all the nodes and antinodes can be represented in the form of the multiple of $n/4$, and so the position of nodes are:

$x = \lambda/4, 3\lambda/4, 5\lambda/4, 7\lambda/4$.............and so on.

and for the position of antinodes here the x becomes:

$x = 0, \lambda/2, \lambda, 3\lambda/2, 2\lambda$................and so on.

The frequency of the wave here is:

$v = nv / 4l$

and the wavelength of the stationary waves is:

$\lambda = 4l / n$

Ratio of the overtones = 1:2:3:4.......all nos. from 1 to ∞

<u>Beats</u>

Have ever heard music? Or more specifically, have you ever heard your voice, or **any Beat**?

Well, yes we heard our voice atleast. So we would be amazed to know that our own voice has various frequency and amplitude having sound waves and they all according to the principal superposition of the waves get superposed and thus somewhere adds up and sometimes gets cancelled out due to certain phase differences. But all in all, we get a superposed wave formed out of different waves of different amplitudes and frequency.

For the sake of simplicity, here we will talk about the waves having the frequency different and other all terms common in them them. So for defining a beat, we tell it as the regular variation of the intensity of the wave with accordance to time and angular frequency, at a particular position due to the superposition of sound waves with slightly different frequencies is called as a **Beat**. Here we consider two sound waves of frequencies v. and v.. , thus having ω. and ω.. .

So we get the equations of the sound waves as

$y. = a\sin(\omega. t) = a\sin(2\pi v. t)$......for wave 1

$y.. = a\sin(\omega.. t) = a\sin(2\pi v.. t)$........for wave 2

Y resultant = y. + y.. ....applying principle of superposition of waves

we obtain,

Y resultant = a sin (2πv. t) + a sin (2πv.. t)

Or,

Y resultant = 2 a sin πt(v. + v..) cos πt(v. - v..) .....[applying sin a + sin b = 2 {sin(a+b)/2 } {cos (a-b)/2}]

Now, we want the beat frequency and for that we need the beat's period. So, for that we consider the following graph.

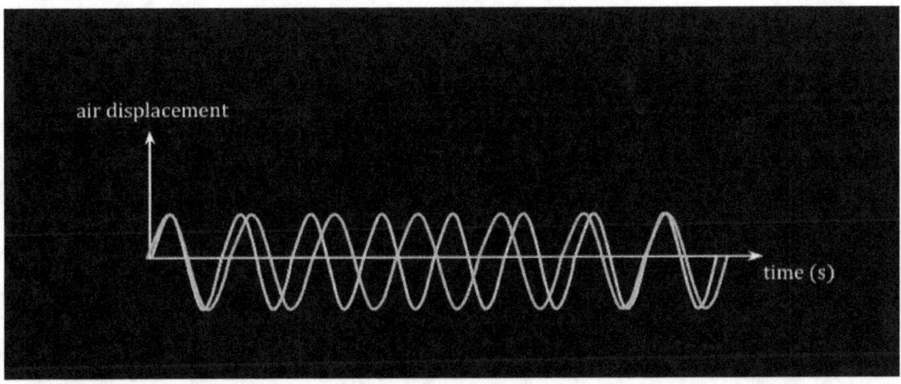

Here we see that after every time period T. the red wave completes one cycle and for the blue wave the time period taken is T.. . We also see that when the waves start being out of phase the difference between T. and T.. increases and then after a no. of cycle of the red wave they again come back and thus are in phase again. Moreover after a certain no. of cycles of the red wave, the blue wave meet up at a point on the graph, i.e T.. . So, we get two equations which are,

ΔT = T. - T..

and,

T.. = n ΔT

Also n= time of the beat to return to 0 phase starting from 0 phase/ Time period of the red wave in one cycle

Or,

n= t/T.

So we get,

T.. = (t/T.) (ΔT) ....[∵ n= t/ T.]

=> T.. T. / ΔT = t

=> t = T.. T. / (T. - T..)

=> t = 1/ {(T.-T..)/T. T..}

=> t = 1/ {(1/ T..) - (1/T.)}

=> t = 1/ {|(v..) - (v.)|}...............Beat Time period

=> v = | v.. - v. | ....Beat Frequency

<u>DOPPLER EFFECT</u>

Consider a sound detector and another sound source. They are fixed at a position and are at rest relative to each other and so the frequency remains constant. But as we detect any movement in the source and/ or the detector we get to know that the frequency starts changing! and obviously with respect to the medium too. Seperated by a distance; when a source of sound and observer, or the source, or the observer, is in motion relative to the medium then there is certain change observed in the frequency of the sound wave so produced, this phenomenon of the change of the frequency of the wave is named as 'The Doppler Effect'.

- **<u>For the Source moving towards/away the Receptor/Observer/Sound detector</u>**

When the source is moving towards Receptor/Observer/Sound detector time required by the first pulse of sound is x/v and that by the second pulse is x-uT/v where u is velocity of the frame and T is the time period in which it covered a certain distance and v is the speed of the sound wave at STP generally. Therefore, time interval T. between the second and the first pulse is,

T. = T + (x-uT/v) - (x/v)

Or,

T. = T(1- u/v)

we know that ,

T. = 1/ v.

and,

T = 1/ v

and so,

T. = T(1- u/v)

=> T. = T((v- u)/v)

=> v. = v [v/v-u]......where v. is the new frequency of the sound wave and v is the initial frequency f the sound wave. here the u should be less than v, otherwise v. will become indefined.

Similarly, when the source is moving away from the observer or recedes from it then it becomes:

v. = v [v/v+u]......where v. is the new frequency of the sound wave and v is the initial frequency f the sound wave.

- ### For the Receptor/Observer/Sound detector moving towards/away the source

Here in this case the first pulse is received in x/v time and the second pulse in T. +((uT. - x) / v) time, where u is the velocity of the Receptor/Observer/Sound detector and the other symbols are T. - the time from Receptor/Observer/Sound detector's frame and T - the time in the source's frame, and v as usual is the sound wave's speed, and, also the Receptor/Observer/Sound detector is moving in the negative x direction.

So, now the Time interval in the Receptor/Observer/Sound detector is:

T = (x/v) + T. +((uT. - x) / v)

=> T = T. ((v+u)/v)

=> T. = vT/ (v+u)

And as we know that,

T. = 1/ v.

and,

T = 1/ v

So,

v. = v (v+u)/v

Hence we now , can derive a general equation for the doppler effect as to be:

v. = v (v ± u.)/(v ∓ u..)

v. = v (v ± u. ± u...)/(v ∓ u.. ± u...)

Where u. is the velocity of the observer, u.. is the velocity of the source and u... is the velocity of the medium which is moving along with them. And, if the medium is moving and the source and of observer is zero, then it doesn't have any impact on the sound wave's frequency so produced. In a similar way appropriate calculations and derivation must be done for the wavelength change in the 'Doppler Effect '.

- **Remember** it's due to the frame of reference which we are choosing and hence the sound wave still vibrates with v Frequency, thus it's due to the movement of the either frames or even both the frames which cause the observation to be different.

Some Concepts You Will Get Interested In

1. Raman Effect

Raman scattering or the Raman effect is the inelastic scattering of photons by matter, meaning that there is both an exchange of energy and a change in the light's direction. Typically this effect involves vibrational energy being gained by a molecule as incident photons from a visible laser are shifted to lower energy. This is called normal Stokes Raman scattering. The effect is exploited by chemists and physicists to gain information about materials for a variety of purposes by performing various forms of Raman spectroscopy. Many other variants of Raman spectroscopy allow rotational energy to be examined (if gas samples are used) and electronic energy levels may be examined if an X-ray source is used in addition to other possibilities. More complex techniques involving pulsed lasers, multiple laser beams and so on are known.

Light has a certain probability of being scattered by a material. When photons are scattered, most of them are elastically scattered (Rayleigh scattering), such that the scattered photons have the same energy (frequency, wavelength and color) as the incident photons but different direction. Rayleigh scattering usually has an intensity in the range 0.1% to 0.01% relative to that of a radiation source. An even smaller fraction of the scattered photons (approximately 1 in 10 million) can be scattered inelastically, with the scattered photons having an energy different (usually lower) from those of the incident photons—these are Raman scattered photons. Because of conservation of energy, the material either gains or loses energy in the process.

The Raman effect is named after Indian scientist C. V. Raman, who discovered it in 1928 with assistance from his student K. S. Krishnan. Raman was awarded the Nobel prize in Physics in 1930 for his discovery. The effect had been predicted theoretically by Adolf Smekal in 1923.

Modern Raman spectroscopy nearly always involves the use of lasers as an exciting light source. Because lasers were not available until more than three decades after the discovery of the effect, Raman and Krishnan used a mercury lamp and photographic plates to record spectra. Early spectra took hours or even days to acquire due to weak light sources, poor sensitivity of the detectors and the weak Raman scattering cross-sections of most materials. The most common modern detectors are charge-coupled devices

(CCDs). Photodiode arrays and photomultiplier tubes were common prior to the adoption of CCDs.

The following focuses on the theory of normal (non-resonant, spontaneous, vibrational) Raman scattering of light by discrete molecules. X-ray Raman spectroscopy is conceptually similar but involves excitation of electronic, rather than vibrational, energy levels.

1.1 Molecular vibrations

Raman scattering generally gives information about vibrations within a molecule. In the case of gases, information about rotational energy can also be gleaned. For solids, phonon modes may also be observed.The basics of infrared absorption regarding molecular vibrations apply to Raman scattering although the selection rules are different.

1.2 Degrees of freedom

For any given molecule, there are a total of 3N degrees of freedom, where N is the number of atoms. This number arises from the ability of each atom in a molecule to move in three dimensions. When dealing with molecules, it is more common to consider the movement of the molecule as a whole. Consequently, the 3N degrees of freedom are partitioned into molecular translational, rotational, and vibrational motion. Three of the degrees of freedom correspond to translational motion of the molecule as a whole (along each of the three spatial dimensions). Similarly, three degrees of freedom correspond to rotations of the molecule about the x,y and z-axes. Linear molecules only have two rotations because rotations along the bond axis do not change the positions of the atoms in the molecule. The remaining degrees of freedom correspond to molecular vibrational modes. These modes include stretching and bending motions of the chemical bonds of the molecule. For a linear molecule, the number of vibrational modes is 3N-5, whereas for a non-linear molecule the number of vibrational modes is 3N-6.

1.3 Vibrational energy

Molecular vibrational energy is known to be quantized and can be modeled using the quantum harmonic oscillator (QHO) approximation or a Dunham expansion when anharmonicity is important. The vibrational energy levels according to the QHO are

$$E = h\left(\frac{2n+1}{2}\right)v = h\left(\frac{2n+1}{2}\right)\left(\frac{1}{2\pi}\right)\left(\sqrt{k/m}\right)$$

where h is the Planck's constant ($h = 6.66 * 10^{-33}$ J s) , n is a quantum number, k is the boltzmann constant($k \approx 8.6 * 10^{-5}$ eV/K)and m is the mass . Since the selection rules for Raman and infrared absorption generally dictate that only fundamental vibrations are observed, infrared excitation or Stokes Raman excitation results in an energy change of

$$E=h\nu=(h/2\pi)(\sqrt{(k/m)})$$

The energy range for vibrations is in the range of approximately 5 to 3500 cm−1. The fraction of molecules occupying a given vibrational mode at a given temperature follows a Boltzmann distribution. A molecule can be excited to a higher vibrational mode through the direct absorption of a photon of the appropriate energy, which falls in the terahertz or infrared range. This forms the basis of infrared spectroscopy. Alternatively, the same vibrational excitation can be produced by an inelastic scattering process. This is called Stokes Raman scattering, by analogy with the Stokes shift in fluorescence discovered by George Stokes in 1852, with light emission at longer wavelength (now known to correspond to lower energy) than the absorbed incident light. Conceptually similar effects can be caused by neutrons or electrons rather than light. An increase in photon energy which leaves the molecule in a lower vibrational energy state is called anti-Stokes scattering.

2. Black Holes

The idea of a body so massive that even light could not escape was briefly proposed by astronomical pioneer and English clergyman John Michell in a letter published in November 1784. Michell's simplistic calculations assumed such a body might have the same density as the Sun, and concluded that such a body would form when a star's diameter exceeds the Sun's by a factor of 500, and the surface escape velocity exceeds the usual speed of light. Michell correctly noted that such supermassive but non-radiating bodies might be detectable through their gravitational effects on nearby visible bodies. Scholars of the time were initially excited by the proposal that giant but invisible stars might be hiding in plain view, but enthusiasm dampened when the wavelike nature of light became apparent in the early nineteenth century.

If light were a wave rather than a "corpuscle", it is unclear what, if any, influence gravity would have on escaping light waves. Modern physics discredits Michell's notion of a light ray shooting directly from the surface of a supermassive star, being slowed down by the star's gravity, stopping, and then free-falling back to the star's surface.

But now, however we have concluded to the fact that there is black hole which can be defined as a region of spacetime where gravity is so strong that nothing—no particles or even electromagnetic radiation such as light—can escape from it. The theory of general relativity predicts that a sufficiently compact mass can deform spacetime to form a black hole. The boundary of no escape is called the event horizon. Although it has an enormous effect on the fate and circumstances of an object crossing it, according to general relativity it has no locally detectable features. In many ways, a black hole acts like an ideal black body, as it reflects no light. Moreover, quantum field theory in curved spacetime predicts that event horizons emit Hawking radiation, with the same spectrum as a black body of a temperature inversely proportional to its mass. This temperature is on the order of billionths of a kelvin for black holes of stellar mass, making it essentially impossible to observe directly.

Objects whose gravitational fields are too strong for light to escape were first considered in the 18th century by John Michell and Pierre-Simon Laplace. The first modern solution of general relativity that would characterize a black hole was found by Karl Schwarzschild in 1916, and its interpretation as a region of space from which nothing can escape was first published by David Finkelstein in 1958. Black holes were long considered a mathematical curiosity; it was not until the 1960s that theoretical work showed they were a generic prediction of general relativity. The discovery of neutron stars by Jocelyn Bell Burnell in 1967 sparked interest in gravitationally collapsed compact objects as a possible astrophysical reality. The first black hole known as such was Cygnus X-1, identified by several researchers independently in 1971.

Black holes of stellar mass form when very massive stars collapse at the end of their life cycle. After a black hole has formed, it can continue to grow by absorbing mass from its surroundings. By absorbing other stars and merging with other black holes, supermassive black holes of millions of solar masses ($M\odot$) may form. There is consensus that supermassive black holes exist in the centers of most galaxies.

The presence of a black hole can be inferred through its interaction with other matter and with electromagnetic radiation such as visible light. Matter that falls onto a black hole can form an external accretion disk heated by friction, forming quasars, some of the brightest objects in the universe. Stars passing too close to a supermassive black hole can be shred into streamers that shine very brightly before being "swallowed." If there are other stars orbiting a black hole, their orbits can be used to determine the black hole's mass and location. Such observations can be used to exclude possible alternatives such as neutron stars. In this way, astronomers have identified numerous stellar black hole candidates in binary systems, and established that the radio source known as Sagittarius A*, at the core of the Milky Way galaxy, contains a supermassive black hole of about 4.3 million solar masses.

On 11 February 2016, the LIGO Scientific Collaboration and the Virgo collaboration announced the first direct detection of gravitational waves, which also represented the first observation of a black hole merger. As of December 2018, eleven gravitational wave events have been observed that originated from ten merging black holes (along with one binary neutron star merger). On 10 April 2019, the first direct image of a black hole and its vicinity was published, following observations made by the Event Horizon Telescope (EHT) in 2017 of the supermassive black hole in Messier 87's galactic centre. In March 2021, the EHT Collaboration presented, for the first time, a polarized-based image of the black hole which may help better reveal the forces giving rise to quasars.

The supermassive black hole at the core of supergiant elliptical galaxy Messier 87, with a mass about 7 billion times that of the Sun, as depicted in the first false-colour image in radio waves released by the Event Horizon Telescope (10 April 2019). Visible are the crescent-shaped emission ring and central shadow, which are gravitationally magnified views of the black hole's photon ring and the photon capture zone of its event horizon. The crescent shape arises from the black hole's rotation and relativistic beaming; the shadow is about 2.6 times the diameter of the event horizon.

Simulation of gravitational lensing by a black hole, which distorts the image of a galaxy in the background

Gas cloud being ripped apart by black hole at the centre of the Milky Way (observations from 2006, 2010 and 2013 are shown in blue, green and red, respectively).

As of 2021, the nearest known body thought to be a black hole is around 1500 light-years away (see List of nearest black holes). Though only a couple dozen black holes have been found so far in the Milky Way, there are thought to be hundreds of millions, most of which are solitary and do not cause emission of radiation, so would only be detectable by gravitational lensing.

3. White Holes

The possibility of the existence of white holes was put forward by Russian cosmologist Igor Novikov in 1964. White holes are predicted as part of a solution to the Einstein field equations known as the maximally extended version of the Schwarzschild metric[clarification needed] describing an eternal black hole with no charge and no rotation. Here, "maximally extended" refers to the idea that the spacetime should not have any "edges": for any possible trajectory of a free-falling particle (following a geodesic) in the spacetime, it should be possible to continue this path arbitrarily far into the particle's future, unless the trajectory hits a gravitational singularity like the one at the center of the black hole's interior. In order to satisfy this requirement, it turns out that in addition to the black hole interior region that particles enter when they fall through the event horizon from the outside, there must be a separate white hole interior region, which allows us to extrapolate the trajectories of particles that an outside observer sees rising up away from the event horizon. For an observer outside using Schwarzschild coordinates, infalling particles take an infinite time to reach the black hole horizon infinitely far in the future, while outgoing particles that pass the observer have been traveling outward for an infinite time since crossing the white hole horizon infinitely far in the past (however, the particles or other objects experience only a finite proper time between crossing the horizon and passing the outside observer). The black hole/white hole appears "eternal" from the perspective of an outside observer, in the sense that particles traveling outward from the white hole interior region can pass the observer at any time, and particles traveling inward, which will eventually reach the black hole interior region can also pass the observer at any time.

Just as there are two separate interior regions of the maximally extended spacetime, there are also two separate exterior regions, sometimes called two different "universes", with the second universe allowing us to extrapolate some possible particle trajectories in the two interior regions. This means that the interior black-hole region can contain a mix of particles that fell in from either universe (and thus an observer who fell in from one universe might be able to see light that fell in from the other one), and likewise particles from the interior white-hole region can escape into either universe. All four regions can be seen in a spacetime diagram that uses Kruskal–Szekeres coordinates (see figure).

In this spacetime, it is possible to come up with coordinate systems such that if you pick a hypersurface of constant time (a set of points that all have the same time coordinate, such that every point on the surface has a space-like separation, giving what is called a 'space-like surface') and draw an "embedding diagram" depicting the curvature of space at that time, the embedding diagram will look like a tube connecting the two exterior regions, known as an "Einstein-Rosen bridge" or Schwarzschild wormhole.Depending on where the space-like hypersurface is chosen, the Einstein-Rosen bridge can either connect two black hole event horizons in each universe (with points in the interior of the bridge being part of the black hole region of the spacetime), or two white hole event horizons in each universe (with points in the interior of the bridge being part of the white hole region). It is impossible to use the bridge to cross from one universe to the other, however, because it is impossible to enter a white hole event horizon from the outside, and anyone entering a black hole horizon from either universe will inevitably hit the black hole singularity.

Note that the maximally extended Schwarzschild metric describes an idealized black hole/white hole that exists eternally from the perspective of external observers; a more realistic black hole that forms at some particular time from a collapsing star would require a different metric. When the infalling stellar matter is added to a diagram of a black hole's history, it removes the part of the diagram corresponding to the white hole interior region. But because the equations of general relativity are time-reversible – they exhibit Time reversal symmetry – general relativity must also allow the time-reverse of this type of "realistic" black hole that forms from collapsing matter. The time-reversed case would be a white hole that has existed since the beginning of the universe, and that emits matter until it finally "explodes" and disappears. Despite the fact that such objects are permitted theoretically, they are not taken as seriously as black holes by physicists, since there would be no processes that would naturally lead to their formation; they could exist only if they were built into the initial conditions of the Big Bang. Additionally, it is predicted that such a white hole would be highly "unstable" in the sense that if any small amount of matter fell towards the horizon from the outside, this would prevent the white hole's explosion as seen by distant observers, with the matter emitted from the singularity never able to escape the white hole's gravitational radius.

In general relativity, a white hole is a hypothetical region of spacetime and singularity that cannot be entered from the outside, although energy-matter, light and information can escape from it. In this sense, it is the reverse of a black hole, which can be entered only from the outside and from which energy-matter, light and information cannot escape. White holes appear in the theory of eternal black holes. In addition to a black hole region in the future, such a solution of the Einstein field equations has a white hole region in its past. This region does not exist for black holes that have formed through gravitational collapse, however, nor are there any observed physical processes through which a white hole could be formed. Supermassive black holes (SBHs) are theoretically predicted to be at the center of every galaxy and that possibly, a galaxy cannot form without one. Stephen Hawking and others have proposed that these SBHs spawn a supermassive white hole/Big Bang.

Like black holes, white holes have properties like mass, charge, and angular momentum. They attract matter like any other mass, but objects falling towards a white hole would never actually reach the white hole's event horizon (though in the case of the maximally extended Schwarzschild solution, discussed below, the white hole event horizon in the past becomes a black hole event horizon in the future, so any object falling towards it will eventually reach the black hole horizon). Imagine a gravitational field, without a surface. Acceleration due to gravity is the greatest on the surface of any body. But since black holes lack a surface, acceleration due to gravity increases exponentially, but never reaches a final value as there is no considered surface in a singularity.In quantum mechanics, the black hole emits Hawking radiation and so it can come to thermal equilibrium with a gas of radiation (not compulsory). Because a thermal-equilibrium state is time-reversal-invariant, Stephen Hawking argued that the time reversal of a black hole in thermal equilibrium results in a white hole in thermal equilibrium (each absorbing and emitting energy to equivalent degrees). Consequently, this may imply that black holes and white holes are the same structure, wherein the Hawking radiation from an ordinary black hole is identified with a white hole's emission of energy and matter. Hawking's semi-classical argument is reproduced in a quantum mechanical AdS/CFT treatment, where a black hole in anti-de Sitter space is described by a thermal gas in a gauge theory, whose time reversal is the same as itself.

Articles

1. Discovery of 10 faces of plasma leads to new insights in fusion and plasma science

Scientists have discovered a novel way to classify magnetized plasmas that could possibly lead to advances in harvesting on Earth the fusion energy that powers the sun and stars. The discovery by theorists at the U.S. Department of Energy's (DOE) Princeton Plasma Physics Laboratory (PPPL) found that a magnetized plasma has 10 unique phases and the transitions between them might hold rich implications for practical development. The spatial boundaries, or transitions, between different phases will support localized wave excitations, the researchers found. "These findings could lead to possible applications of these exotic excitations in space and laboratory plasmas," said Yichen Fu, a graduate student at PPPL and lead author of a paper in Nature Communications that outlines the research. "The next step is to explore what these excitations could do and how they might be utilized."

Possible applications

Possible applications include using the excitations to create current in magnetic fusion plasmas or facilitating plasma rotation in fusion experiments. However, "Our paper doesn't consider any practical applications," said physicist Hong Qin, co-author of the paper and Fu's advisor. "The paper is the basic theory and the technology will follow the theoretical understanding." In fact, "the discovery of the 10 phases in plasma marks a primary development in plasma physics," Qin said. "The first and foremost step in any scientific endeavor is to classify the objects under investigation. Any new classification scheme will lead to improvement in our theoretical understanding and subsequent advances in technology," he said. Qin cites discovery of the major types of diabetes as an example of the role classification plays in scientific progress. "When developing treatments for diabetes, scientists found that there were three major types," he said. "Now medical practitioners can effectively treat diabetic patients." Fusion, which scientists around the world are seeking to produce on Earth, combines light elements in the form of plasma -- the hot, charged state of matter composed of free electrons and atomic nuclei that makes up 99 percent of the visible universe -- to release massive amounts of energy. Such energy could serve as a safe and clean source of power for generating electricity. The plasma phases that PPPL has uncovered are technically known as "topological phases," indicating the shapes of the waves supported by plasma. This unique property of matter was first discovered in the discipline of condensed matter physics during the 1970s -- a discovery for which physicist Duncan Haldane of Princeton University shared the 2016 Nobel Prize for his pioneering work.

Robust and intrinsic

The localized plasma waves produced by phase transitions are robust and intrinsic because they are "topologically protected," Qin said. "The discovery that this topologically protected excitation exists in magnetized plasmas is a big step forward that can be explored for practical applications," he said. For first author Fu, "The most important progress in the paper is looking at plasma based on its topological properties and identifying its topological phases. Based on these phases we identify the necessary and sufficient condition for the excitations of these localized waves. As for how this progress can be applied to facilitate fusion energy research, we have to find out."

2. Scientists develop world's thinnest magnet

Scientists in the US have developed an ultrathin magnet that operates at room temperature. They believe it could lead to new applications in computing and electronics and new tools for the study of quantum physics. According to the researchers, the magnet could make advances in next-gen memories, computing, spintronics – such as high-density, compact spintronic memory devices – and quantum physics. It was developed by scientists at the Department of Energy's Lawrence Berkeley National Laboratory (Berkeley Lab) and UC Berkeley. "We're the first to make a room-temperature 2D magnet that is chemically stable under ambient conditions," said senior author Jie Yao, a faculty scientist in Berkeley Lab's Materials Sciences Division and associate professor of materials science and engineering at UC Berkeley. Graduate student at UC Berkeley, Rui Chen, added: "This discovery is exciting because it not only makes 2D magnetism possible at room temperature, but it also uncovers a new mechanism to realise 2D magnetic materials." . The magnetic component of today's memory devices is typically made of magnetic thin films. But at the atomic level, these magnetic films are still three-dimensional – hundreds or thousands of atoms thick. For decades, researchers have searched for ways to make thinner and smaller 2D magnets and thus enable data to be stored at a much higher density. Previous achievements in 2D magnetic materials have brought promising results. But these early 2D magnets lose their magnetism and become chemically unstable at room temperature, according to experts. "State-of-the-art 2D magnets need very low temperatures to function. But for practical reasons, a data centre needs to run at room temperature," Yao said. "Theoretically, we know that the smaller the magnet, the larger the disc's potential data density. Our 2D magnet is not only the first that operates at room temperature or higher, but it is also the first magnet to reach the true 2D limit: It's as thin as a single atom!". The researchers said their discovery will also enable new opportunities to study quantum physics. "Our atomically thin magnet offers an optimal platform for probing the quantum world," Yao said. "It opens up every single atom for examination, which may reveal how quantum physics governs each single magnetic atom and the interactions between them. With a conventional bulk magnet where most of the magnetic atoms are deeply buried inside the material, such studies would be quite challenging to do."

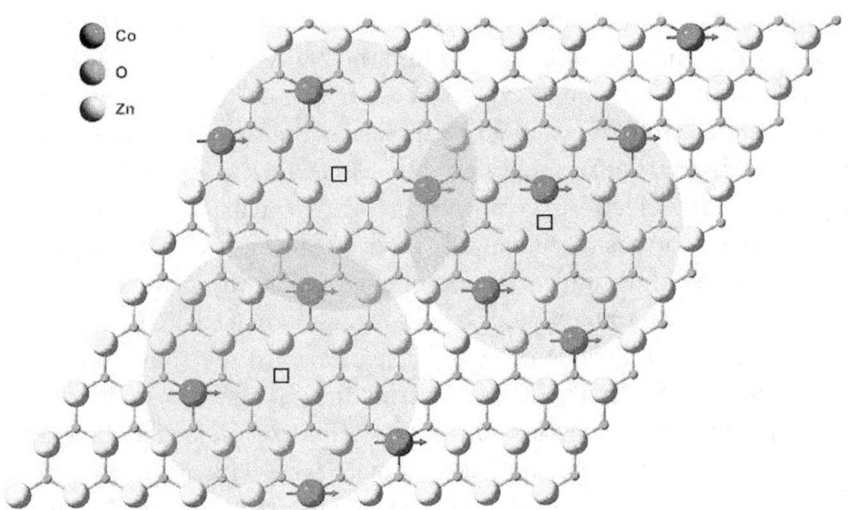

Fig.1 - Illustration of magnetic coupling in a cobalt-doped zinc-oxide monolayer. Red, blue, and yellow spheres represent cobalt, oxygen, and zinc atoms, respectively.

The researchers synthesised the new 2D magnet – called a cobalt-doped van der Waals zinc-oxide magnet – from a solution of graphene oxide, zinc, and cobalt. Just a few hours of baking in a conventional lab oven transformed the mixture into a single atomic layer of zinc oxide with a smattering of cobalt atoms sandwiched between layers of graphene. In a final step, graphene is burned away, leaving behind just a single atomic layer of cobalt-doped zinc oxide. To confirm that the resulting 2D film is just one atom thick, Yao and his team conducted scanning electron microscopy experiments at Berkeley Lab's Molecular Foundry to identify the material's morphology, and transmission electron microscopy imaging to probe the material atom by atom. With proof in hand that their 2D material really is just an atom thick, the researchers went on to the next challenge that had confounded researchers for years: demonstrating a 2D magnet that successfully operates at room temperature. The research team's lab experiments showed that the graphene-zinc-oxide system becomes weakly magnetic with a 5-6 per cent concentration of cobalt atoms. Increasing the concentration of cobalt atoms to about 12 per cent results in a powerful magnet. They also found that a concentration of cobalt atoms exceeding 15 per cent shifts the 2D magnet into an exotic quantum state of "frustration," whereby different magnetic states within the 2D system compete with each other. And unlike previous 2D magnets, which lose their magnetism at room temperature or above, the researchers found that the new 2D magnet not only works at room temperature but also at 100°C. According to Chen, zinc oxide's free electrons could act as an intermediary that ensures the magnetic cobalt atoms in the new 2D device continue pointing in the same direction – and thus stay magnetic – even when the host, in this case, the semiconductor zinc oxide, is a non-magnetic material. "Free electrons are constituents of electric currents. They move in the same direction to conduct electricity," Yao added, comparing the movement of free electrons in metals and semiconductors to the flow of water molecules in a stream of water. The researchers say that new material – which can be bent into almost any shape without breaking and is one millionth the thickness of a single sheet of paper – could help advance the application of spin electronics or spintronics, a new technology that uses the orientation of an electron's spin rather than its charge to encode data. "Our 2D magnet may enable the formation of ultra-compact spintronic devices to engineer the spins of the electrons," Chen said.

3. New mechanism of superconductivity discovered in graphene

Placing a 2D Bose-Einstein condensate in the vicinity of a graphene layer confers superconductivity to the material.

Superconductivity is a physical phenomenon where the electrical resistance of a material drops to zero under a certain critical temperature. Bardeen-Cooper-Schrieffer (BCS) theory is a well-established explanation that describes superconductivity in most materials. It states that Cooper pairs of electrons are formed in the lattice under sufficiently low temperature and that BCS superconductivity arises from their condensation. While graphene itself is an excellent conductor of electricity, it does not exhibit BCS superconductivity due to the suppression of electron-phonon interactions. This is also the reason that most 'good' conductors such as gold and copper are 'bad' superconductors. Researchers at the Center for Theoretical Physics of Complex Systems (PCS), within the Institute for Basic Science (IBS, South Korea) have reported on a novel alternative mechanism to achieve superconductivity in graphene. They achieved this feat by proposing a hybrid system consisting of graphene and 2D Bose-Einstein condensate (BEC). This research is published in the journal 2D Materials. Along with superconductivity, BEC is another phenomenon that arises at low temperatures. It is the fifth state of matter first predicted by Einstein in 1924. The formation of BEC occurs when low-energy atoms clump together and enter the same energy state, and it is an area that is widely studied in condensed matter physics. A hybrid Bose-Fermi system essentially represents a layer of electrons interacting with a layer of bosons, such as indirect excitons, exciton-polaritons, etc. The interaction between Bose and Fermi particles leads to various novel fascinating phenomena, which piques interests from both the fundamental and application-oriented perspectives. In this work, the researchers report a new mechanism of superconductivity in graphene, which arises due to interactions between electrons and "bogolons," rather than phonons as in typical BCS systems. Bogolons, or Bogoliubov quasiparticles, are excitation within BEC which has some characteristics of a particle. In certain ranges of parameters, this mechanism permits the critical temperature for superconductivity up to 70 Kelvin within graphene. The researchers also developed a new microscopic BCS theory which focuses specifically on the novel hybrid graphene-based system. Their proposed model also predicts that superconducting properties can be enhanced with temperature, resulting in the non-monotonous temperature dependence of the superconducting gap. Furthermore, the research showed that the Dirac dispersion of graphene is preserved in this bogolon-mediated scheme. This indicates that this superconducting mechanism involves electrons with relativistic dispersion -- a phenomenon that is not so well-explored in condensed matter physics. "This work sheds light on an alternative way to achieve high-temperature superconductivity. Meanwhile, by controlling the properties of a condensate, we can tune the superconductivity of graphene. This suggests another channel to control the superconductor devices in the future.," explains Ivan Savenko, the leader of the Light-Matter Interaction in Nanostructures (LUMIN) team at the PCS IBS.

3. Star Trek's Warp Drive Leads to New Physics
Researchers are taking a closer look at this science-fiction
staple—and bringing the idea a little closer to reality

For Erik Lentz, it all started with Star Trek. Every few episodes of Star Trek: The Next Generation, Captain Jean-Luc Picard would raise his hand and order, "Warp one, engage!" Then stars became dashes, and light-years flashed by at impossible speed. And Lentz, still in elementary school, wondered whether warp drive might also work in real life.

"At some point, I realized that the technology didn't exist," Lentz says. He studied physics at the University of Washington, wrote his Ph.D. dissertation on dark matter and generally became far too busy to be concerned with science fiction. But then, at the start of the coronavirus pandemic, Lentz found himself alone in Göttingen, Germany, where he was doing postdoctoral work. He suddenly had plenty of free time on his hands—and childhood fancies in his head.

Lentz read everything he could find on warp drives in the scientific literature, which was not very much. Then he began to think about it for himself. After a few weeks, something occurred to him that everyone else seemed to have overlooked. Lentz put his idea on paper and discussed it with more experienced colleagues. A year later it was published in a physics journal.

It quickly became clear that Lentz was not the only person dreaming about warp drives. Media outlets all over the world picked up the story, and a dozen journalists asked for interviews. A discussion on the online forum Reddit attracted 2,700 comments and 33,000 likes. One Internet user wrote, "Anyone else feel like they were born 300 years too soon?"

A BUBBLE IN SPACE AND TIME

There is no doubt that the universe is still far too vast for humans to traverse. It takes more than four years for a beam of light to reach Earth's nearest star Proxima Centauri. Even with the best available propulsion systems, it would take tens of thousands of years for a human to get there. One can always dream about establishing colonies in other star systems, but it is not a journey anyone is likely to undertake.

But perhaps one day it might be possible to reduce the travel time. There are many ideas about how to do that, from laser-accelerated solar sails to nuclear propulsion. But even with the aid of these technologies, you would not get too far in a human lifetime. The galaxy really is open only to those who travel as fast as light—or faster.

Fig.2 NASA artist's 1998 rendition of warp drive travel. The ring around the spacecraft generates a negative-energy field. From today's perspective, the negative-energy field would no longer be necessary. Credit: NASA; Digital art by Les Bossinas (Cortez III Service Corp)

For that very reason, imaginative physicists have long been pondering the ultimate propulsion system: a bubble in space and time in which a spaceship could dash from sun to sun, just like the USS Enterprise did. This is research at the fringe of science: not necessarily wrong but spiced with a large pinch of optimism.

The fact that scientists are dealing with the idea at all today is thanks to a 1994 paper by Mexican theoretical physicist Miguel Alcubierre. At the time, Alcubierre was not just a passionate Star Trek devotee. In his doctoral thesis at the University of Wales College Cardiff (now Cardiff University), Alcubierre also worked on the theory of relativity. Strictly speaking, the theory states that nothing can travel faster than light. But by applying a little creativity, Alcubierre identified an apparent loophole.

For physicists, Albert Einstein's theory of relativity consists of two parts: The "special" theory of relativity, which dates from 1905, deals with the uniform motion of fast-as-light objects. Ten years later Einstein generalized these ideas for accelerating bodies. According to "general" relativity, the three spatial dimensions we are familiar with (up-down, left-right, front-back) are inseparable from time. Every mass deforms this spacetime.

According to Albert Einstein's epic discovery, we live in four-dimensional "spacetime." Spacetime is not static. Like a tablecloth, it is deformed by massive objects. Everything that moves across the tablecloth (or through spacetime) can accelerate only up to the speed limit set by light. The tablecloth itself, on the other hand, can be deformed at any speed, as the universe itself shows in some situations.

At the instant of the big bang, for example, the original spacetime structure presumably expanded for a split second and did so much faster than any ray of light could travel. Even today, the expansion continues to drive extremely distant galaxies away at speeds faster than light, which means their light can no longer reach us.

Based on his discovery, Alcubierre surmised that it would only be a small step to a warp drive. If spacetime were contracted in front of a spaceship and expanded behind it to compensate, it would be possible to travel to one's destination at a speed faster than light. The ship would remain encapsulated in a bubble, and the crew would not sense the magnitude of the interstellar journey. In a 2017 lecture, Alcubierre compared it to being on a passenger conveyor belt at the airport: "You can imagine that the floor behind you is being created out of nothing and in front of you it is being destroyed, so you move along."

But formulating this idea in the language of general relativity immediately gives rise to major practical problems. First, to deform spacetime so radically, you would need to cram a huge mass into a bubble bounded by a wall thinner than an atomic nucleus. Then you would need two forms of matter to maintain the bubble. The gravity of ordinary mass would cause the space at the front of the bubble to contract, moving the whole structure forward. But at the same time, the space at the back of the bubble would need to expand like rising bread dough. To make that expansion happen, according to Alcubierre, you would need some form of negative energy radiating a kind of antigravity.

THE CURSE OF NEGATIVE ENERGY

For most physicists, that was the end of the thought experiment. Energy—which according to Einstein's formula $E = mc^2$ is equivalent to unconstrained mass—seems like it must, by definition, be positive. But according to quantum theory, it can indeed have a negative value. This seems to occur only in rare special cases, however—on a tiny scale. In the so-called Casimir effect, for example, the quantities involved are so minuscule that any technological application seems absurd.

Alcubierre, now a professor of physics at the National Autonomous University of Mexico, concedes this point. In terms of a potential technology, warp drives "are greatly lacking," he and one of his colleagues wrote in a recent preprint paper. He has now turned his attention to known phenomena, such as black holes. The warp drive concept, however, retains its fascination, especially for Trekkies—and for a few gravitational physicists, who occasionally publish variations on the idea.

Some of these papers have shown how to reduce the bubble's mass requirements so that the total mass needed to deform spacetime would be less than that of our sun. But no one was able to get around the problem of negative energy—until Lentz took it up during the lockdown in Göttingen. In his enforced isolation, Lentz found a way to construct a warp bubble using only positive energy. In so doing, he may have overcome the greatest objection to warp drives.

What made it possible was a special feature of the geometry of spacetime that Lentz discovered buried in the general theory of relativity—more precisely, in Einstein's field equations. These equations can calculate how a particular distribution of matter and energy deforms spacetime. Researchers can also use them, as Alcubierre did, to determine the mass and energy needed to produce a specific curvature of space.

Dealing with a dynamic, four-dimensional structure like spacetime is extremely complicated, however. Writing out Einstein's formulas in full produces a jumble of nested differential equations with thousands of terms.

Depending on the assumptions you make about a particular physical situation, you only take some of those terms into account. For theorists, it is an almost limitless playground.

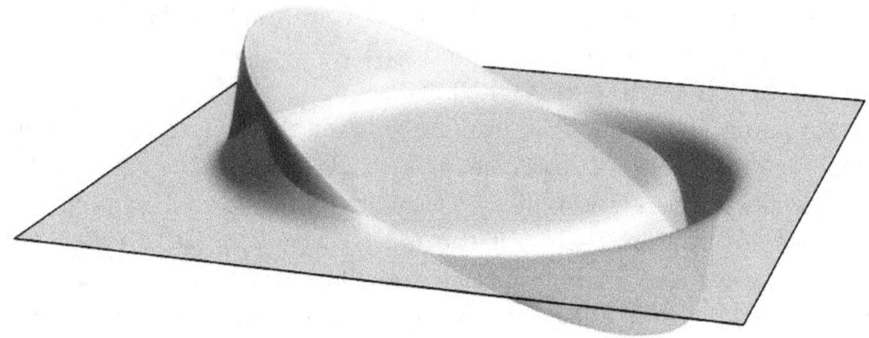

Fig. 3 Principle of the Alcubierre drive: Spacetime contracts at the front of the bubble (right), corresponding to a warp in spacetime. Behind the bubble (left), new space is created out of nothing, which is equivalent to stretching spacetime. Credit: AllenMcC Wikimedia (CC BY-SA 3.0)

Lentz specifically examined the assumptions leading to the negative energy requirements in Alcubierre's work. Like his colleague, Lentz began by analyzing spacetime, modeling the multidimensional substance as a stack of very thin layers. He found that Alcubierre had only considered comparatively simple "linear" relationships between the equations for shifting one layer onto the next. At this point, choosing more complex "hyperbolic" relations, which typically express rapidly changing quantities, results in a different warp bubble than the one obtained by Alcubierre. It still requires enormous amounts of mass and energy but, according to Lentz's calculations, only positive amounts. "I was very surprised that no one had tried this before me," Lentz says.

Lentz's bubble looks different from the one Alcubierre worked out in 1994. It consists of diamond-shaped regions of altered spacetime that resemble a flock of birds. Creating such a spacetime geometry in reality would involve a complicated layering of rings and disks, not made of solid material but of an extremely dense fluid of charged particles, similar to the substance found in the interior of neutron stars, Lentz says.

That means near-light-speed travel is still very, very far away from applied technology. But now that no exotic negative energy densities are needed—at least according to Lentz's latest work—the theoretical games are within the realm of established physics. Alcubierre describes Lentz's paper as a "very important development." Francisco Lobo, a researcher at the University of Lisbon and a colleague of Alcubierre's, who has published a textbook on warp drives, cannot find any obvious errors either. "If correct, this has the potential of opening up new interest and novel avenues of research in warp drive physics," he says.

Lentz's idea has even aroused interest among researchers outside the small community of warp drive enthusiasts, including Lavinia Heisenberg, a professor of cosmology at the Swiss Federal Institute of Technology Zurich. Heisenberg and her student Shaun Fell found Lentz's paper so exciting that they built on it by designing their own positive-energy warp bubbles that would require as little as a thousandth of the mass of our sun.

"The whole thing is much less mysterious than most people assume," says Alexey Bobrick, an astrophysicist at Lund University in Sweden. Collaborating with New York City–based entrepreneur Gianni Martire, Bobrick came up with some promising solutions to Einstein's field equations in 2020. According to Bobrick, all that is needed for a warp bubble is an appropriately shaped shell made of dense material that bends spacetime in its immediate vicinity while the universe through which the bubble moves and the space within the shell remain comparatively undisturbed.

TIME GOES BY SO SLOWLY

"Comparatively" is the key. Alcubierre and later warp architects assumed an abrupt transition between the contorted spacetime in the wall of the bubble and the smooth interior and exterior. But Bobrick and Martire found this "truncation" of the gravitational field to be the reason why large amounts of negative energy are required to stabilize the contortion of space and time.

Abandoning the cartoonish image of a soap bubble, however, makes it possible to build warp drives based on ordinary matter, they claim. The gravitational field would not simply disappear when one moved away from the wall of the shell. Instead it would gradually decay. Spacetime would therefore also be curved inside the bubble. To travelers in a spaceship right in the middle of the bubble, this phenomenon would be most obvious in the passage of time: their watches would go slower than in the rest of space because, according to the theory of relativity, time is affected by gravity.

The slower passage of time on a spaceship might be something interstellar travelers appreciate. Still, Bobrick and Martire describe other obstacles. So far, they argue, there is no known way to actually accelerate a warp bubble. All previous ideas about the subject simply assume that the curvature of spacetime is already moving at high speed.

A beam of light travels 299,000 kilometers per second. According to Einstein's special theory of relativity, this is a physical constant. The speed of light is the maximum speed any particle may reach, and a particle can only do so if it has no mass. Consequently, today's physics offers no possibility of accelerating objects beyond the speed of light. On closer inspection, however, this limit only applies within the four-dimensional spacetime comprising the universe. Outside of that, even greater speeds appear to be possible.

"None of the physically conceivable warp drives can accelerate to speeds faster than light," Bobrick says. That is because you would require matter capable of being ejected at speeds faster than light—but no known particles can travel that fast. Furthermore, the bubble could not be controlled by occupants of the spaceship itself because they would lose contact with the outside world, owing to the extremely strong curvature of space around them.

Lentz sees these objections as a problem, too, but he believes a solution can be found. Bobrick, meanwhile, points out that it is also possible to travel to distant stars at a third or half the speed of light, especially if time passes more slowly for the people in the warp bubble. Just do not think about the fact that all your relatives left behind on Earth will probably have died of old age before you get back. "But at least the idea is no longer completely crazy," Bobrick says.

FROM THEORY TO PRACTICE

There is still some debate about whether warp bubbles really can do without negative energy. Recently, three theoreticians suggested that this claim was only true for observers moving next to the bubble. Plus, not everything that seems possible according to the theory of relativity actually exists—or is technologically feasible. For example, Einstein's field equations can also be used to justify "white" holes (the antithesis of their black hole counterparts), Einstein-Rosen bridges (frequently called wormholes) and other exotic alterations in spacetime that no one has ever observed. That could be because laws of nature, as yet unknown, preclude such phenomena.

Some researchers therefore caution against going overboard with the fantasies. Space propulsion expert Martin Tajmar of the Technical University of Dresden, for example, sees no practical relevance for the current work on warp drives. The huge masses involved simply exceed anything that can be tested on Earth, he says.

Most veteran warp drive researchers would undoubtedly agree. They see their work less as preparation for real-world experiments and more as a way of exploring the limits of relativity. In this endeavor, even speculative "thought experiments" are useful, Lobo says.

Lentz, on the other hand, is actively working toward a practical application of his idea. After his research in Göttingen, he took a job at an IT company. But in his spare time, he still thinks about how to accelerate a bend in spacetime to speeds faster than light and how to reduce the energy required to do so.

Lentz also advocates looking closely at the surroundings of neutron stars. It could be that these ultracompact stellar remnants eject bubbles like those that he describes in his paper. "As long as one doesn't let personal biases get in the way and accepts what evidence tells you, it's a field of research that is as worthy of being pursued as any other," he says.

Jean-Luc Picard would probably see it similarly. "Things are only impossible until they are not," the character noted in an episode of Star Trek: The Next Generation. But that's also easier to say when you live 300 years in the future.

References

For Part 1- Newtonian Mechanics

Chapter-4 the types of Forces

https://www.clearias.com/four-fundamental-forces-of-nature/ ------last image[Fig.4]

Except above all images are made in *Microsoft Paint*

For Part 2- Heat and Temperature

From___ https://www.toppr.com/ask/content/concept/anomalous-expansion-of-water-210020/

i have referred the second graph inside the topic of **Anomalous expansion of water** in the chapter

7 i.e Thermal Expansion

For part 2 chapter 9, 3.6.1, Wien Displacement law

http://hyperphysics.phy-astr.gsu.edu/hbase/wien.html ------> graph

For part 3 chapter 10,

The Hollow Hole Through The Earth: A Hypothetical concept of SHM, An introduction to Hypothesis

From the part A hypothesis...................recognized knowledge-systems. is taken from the link below

https://en.wikipedia.org/wiki/Hypothesis

For part 3 chapter 12,

Taken picture(Fig.1) from

https://www.researchgate.net/figure/a-A-positive-pulse-produced-on-a-light-string-travels-towards-a-heavier-string-At-the_fig9_257023443

For part 3 chapter 12,

Taken graph of the beat in the 'Beat' section from the youtube link: https://youtu.be/pI6iJg_W1ug

For the chapters 10, 11 and 12 , reference taken from Concepts of Physics volume 1, by H.C.Verma and from NCERT Fingertips of MTG.

For The section of 'Some Concepts You Will Get Interested In'

All the topics have been taken from Wikipedia in this section. For more information on these topics

go to:

en.wikipedia.org, and browse for the topics given in the section......

For Articles section

https://www.sciencedaily.com/releases/2021/07/210712183308.htm is the source for Article 1

https://eandt.theiet.org/content/articles/2021/07/scientists-develop-world-s-thinnest-magnet/ is the source for Article 2

https://www.sciencedaily.com/releases/2021/07/210714110612.htm is the source for Article 3

https://www.scientificamerican.com/article/star-treks-warp-drive-leads-to-new-physics/ is the source for Article 4.

www.ingramcontent.com/pod-product-compliance
Lightning Source LLC
Chambersburg PA
CBHW052031150726
48002CB00002B/544